COMMON SENSE
INCOME STRATEGIES

APPROACHES FOR REACHING YOUR RETIREMENT DESTINATION

MARK FALTER

Mark Falter / Mid-American Wealth Advisory Group
7505 NW Tiffany Springs Parkway, Kansas City, MO 64153
www.midamericanwealthadvisory.com

Book layout ©2022 Advisors Excel, LLC

Common Sense Income Strategies / Mark Falter — 1st edition

ISBN 9798842477029

Mark Falter is registered as an Investment Advisor Representative and is a licensed insurance agent in the state of Missouri. Mid-American Wealth Advisory Group is an independent financial services firm that helps individuals create retirement strategies using a variety of investment and insurance products to custom suit their needs and objectives.

The contents of this book are provided for informational purposes only and are not intended to serve as the basis for any financial decisions. Any tax, legal, or estate planning information is general in nature. It should not be construed as legal or tax advice. Always consult an attorney or tax professional regarding the applicability of this information to your unique situation.

Information presented is believed to be factual and up-to-date, but we do not guarantee its accuracy, and it should not be regarded as a complete analysis of the subjects discussed. All expressions of opinion are those of the author as of the date of publication and are subject to change. Content should not be construed as personalized investment advice nor should it be interpreted as an offer to buy or sell any securities mentioned. A financial advisor should be consulted before implementing any of the strategies presented.

Investing involves risk, including the potential loss of principal. No investment strategy can guarantee a profit or protect against loss in periods of declining values. Any references to protection benefits or guaranteed/lifetime income streams refer only to fixed insurance products, not securities or investment products. Insurance and annuity product guarantees are backed by the financial strength and claims-paying ability of the issuing insurance company.

Any names used in the examples in this book are hypothetical only and do not represent actual clients.

*I dedicate this book to Thomas Falter Sr.
You got me started in this business, and I look forward
to seeing you again.*

Table of Contents

On A Clear Day, You Can Really See Your Future

The view from 5,000 feet above a summer landscape in America is one of the many joys of living in this nation today. I look out the side window of the single-engine Cessna 172 as we make lazy eights in the afternoon sky, embracing that joy, and my part in the health of that landscape below. Earlier I was sitting left chair, piloting this same plane above my chosen homeland of Missouri, honing my own skill and concentration. I now have the privilege to sit back and observe, taking in the beauty and diversity of God's creation all around me.

Below is the mosaic of the America I love. It is the rise of commercial buildings in the city a few miles in the distance, and it is the neatly plowed fields of the farmers who feed those cities. It is the shopping malls and factories, the golf courses, and the gravel quarries. It is the fishermen in the boats on the river, the hikers on the trails.

It is the sprawling grounds of the Purina compound where thousands of people come each year to show their purebred dogs and horses. It is the water slides and roller coasters of Six Flags Amusement Park where families laugh and play together.

It is woodlots and acreage, purchased and set aside for nature preserves and hunting camps. It is herds of deer and fields of quail and pheasants. It is golf courses and country clubs, built and maintained by the collective effort and investment of the members.

It is the interstate highways and backcountry roads, filled with travelers going on vacation or off to work. It is the bridges and tunnels, the fire houses and the police departments, the military bases and the parks and campgrounds. The funding for these projects are often part of the retirement strategies that provide income for the families who have worked for many years.

This American mosaic is the new construction at the Shriner's Children's Hospital—funded by the gifts from caring citizens across this land. It is schools, colleges, universities, trade and vocational schools. It is churches, synagogues, meeting halls, and mosques. It is nursery schools and day care centers, nursing homes and retirement communities.

It is the farmers and the doctors, the lawyers and the judges, the nurses and firemen, the bankers and the brokers, the merchants and the mechanics, the teachers and the students, the artists and the critics, the soldier and the police officer.

It is all of those who work and earn, who save for their retirement and invest in the future of the nation. It is those who spend lives dedicated to careful planning, anticipating the growth of cities, the need for interstate highways connecting population centers, a stable power grid keeping the light on, recharging a new generation of electric vehicles, budgeting for the long-term cost of such projects.

Each morning as the sun rises across America, it is all of us, wanting to ensure a strong, secure, and vibrant nation for our children and grandchildren. As each day begins, I arise, filled with the joy of accomplishment that I have brought to this mosaic. The success of my efforts to help my family of clients plan for their future is reflected in the growth and progress I see around me.

I have dedicated my life to listening carefully to people. People like the grandfather who fishes with his grandchildren on the Meramec River. When he came to me years ago to help prepare for his retirement, we explored his thoughts of an ideal retirement. He wanted to be confident he would have the resources to spend summer afternoons sharing his love of nature with his grandchildren. I enjoy knowing that when the weather is right, that is exactly what he's doing.

In a few short hours, the sun will set, our families and friends will gather and the evening sky will bloom with the bright colors and loud booms of the fireworks celebrating Independence Day. Americans will look to the sky and be reminded that the birth of this nation under the watchful eye of careful planners is a gift to cherish and celebrate. Each day I embrace our shared responsibility to maintain and preserve this 246-year-old gift that is our nation.

Even though we are flying through clear blue sky, with no obvious obstacles or obstructions, the little plane drops through a rough patch of sky where rising air heated by the fields and concrete below encounters cooler air from above, the turbulence of opposing forces rocking the plane side to side. Our pilot gently corrects for crosswinds, maintains a safe altitude, all with a calm assurance and a steady hand.

From the security of the rear seat, I watch the young man who holds my life in his hands. The joke about "flying is easy, it is landing that is hard," comes to mind.

This plane will eventually land. For as surely as every plane has ever lifted into the air, each and every one of them has returned to earth, no assistance is required. The desired outcome is to descend in a planned fashion, aligned to the center of the runway, correcting for wind drift and unexpected events, and settling gently onto the wheels of a smooth touchdown. That safe outcome is dependent upon planning and preparedness, practice, and patience. It is an exact metaphor for the talents I bring to helping clients plan their retirement.

The man holding my life in his hands is the pilot in command, the youngest of my three beloved children, my son Joshua. He holds the controls with a calm authority, adjusting throttle and trim, watching the sky around us for other aircraft. He approaches perfecting his flying skills with the same dedication and enthusiasm he brings to every aspect of his daily life.

Seated next to him is a Certified Flight Instructor, teaching and mentoring Joshua as he guides the plane back to the airport, back to the embrace of our family, back to the familiar assurance of solid ground. Our CFI has thousands of hours of experience, has flown multiple types of aircraft, and has studied the theory and the actuality of mastering the complexities of flight. He too has placed his life, his future in the hands of my son, for if we fail to land safely, we fail together.

On the ground are others who bring their talents and skill to ensuring the success of this flight. There is the mechanic who services the plane, insuring that all is in good working order. There is the air traffic controller, who monitors the position, altitude, direction of travel and proximity of other aircraft in the area.

With sensors and reporting stations around the world, there is the National Weather Service, providing constant monitoring of the wind speed, cloud cover, temperature, humidity, dangerous weather patterns, tornados, and other factors.

There is the Federal Aviation Authority, registering aircraft, recording ownership, tracking safety and performance data, and most importantly, maintaining and enforcing the standards to which every pilot must comply.

The interrelationship of people with different responsibilities, all helping to make safe flight possible works in the same way as the uncountable inputs which maintain a vibrant economy. Those relationships are also critical; each segment must coordinate and work together for the best result —people and projects, savings and investments, planning and designing, wildcatters and regulators. Risk must be identified; practical solutions must be tied to security. Ethics and integrity must never be sacrificed for convenience or profit.

This is the perfect symmetry which engages my place in this mix; it is what defines my lifelong drive to bring my best efforts to all of my clients and to my family.

So I am extending this invitation to each of you to come along with me for a flight into knowledge and understanding. I want to share the lessons my "Certified Flight Instructors" have taught me. I want you and your family to enjoy your flight across our beautiful nation, secure and free of worry about your safe landing.

I want to share with you my experiences, my insights, my hopes for the future. I want your family to enjoy the confidence and security of knowing that your plans and dreams are being treated with the respect, appreciation, and diligence that you deserve.

Our future is ahead of us, come along with me.

CHAPTER 1

A Grounded Upbringing

Just seven years before my parents brought me into this world, or more specifically, Thanksgiving Day of 1958, the snow began falling throughout West Virginia's Northern Panhandle. It has blanketed towns and villages with layer upon layer of white. The slag heaps and coal tips of the steel mill were covered. Rail lines and roadways were buried, traffic slowed to nearly a standstill.

The beauty of newly fallen snow made for an impressive change of pace, covering years of soot and ash from the huge forges in the steel mill. It is just one of many examples, but certainly, the best to allow me to present the driving spirit of the men and women of my hometown of Weirton. As the snow accumulated, the threat to the community grew and eventually became serious.

Traffic came to a halt, power lines went down, even the train tracks were affected, and loads of ore for the smelters and coal to fire the furnaces were blocked. Instinctively the hard working people of Weirton responded.

They did not wait for "somebody to do something." They picked up shovels and moved mountains of snow. They climbed on the roofs of homes and businesses, saving buildings, with their efforts, from collapsing under the weight of the snow.

They removed snow and ice from the roadways so cars, trucks, and buses could reach homes, schools, and hospitals. They adapted equipment from the mill to effectively melt the snow along the railroad tracks so trainloads of ore and coal could resupply the mill and keep operations alive.

Over 1,000 workers were snowed in at the mill; they worked more than seventy-two hours through the storm. Hour after hour, they looked after one another; they worked as their own closed-off community tried to survive.

The people of Weirton took responsibility and cleared roads and driveways to get a new mother and her newborn home. They carried groceries to an older woman shut in at home. Schoolchildren reveled in the fact that school was closed all week, never thinking that their struggle at home was likely even tougher.

It was 1958; this was the spirit and soul of working-class America. These are the values into which I was fortunate to be born just a few years later.

My parents had a small home on Wanda Street in this blue-collar town; I was the youngest of their six children. This was middle-class America with a strong flavor of Norman Rockwell around every turn. Growing up in an environment of blue-collar industries and self-sufficient neighbors gives a child an appreciation for hard work and dedication to the task.

As children, we had chores to complete, lawns to mow, leaves to rake, snow to shovel. We rode American built Schwinn bicycles across town, to school, and to the lake to where we kept an eye on each other as we swam. Neighbors looked after all the children as they played in the empty lots and ball fields.

In our schools, we cleaned blackboard erasers, lined up our desks, raised our hands to answer or ask a question. We started each day with the Pledge of Allegiance, hand over heart, facing our flag, which had pride of place at the front of every classroom.

There was no single, stunning moment when I became aware of the culture of Middle America into which I was born. There were segments of time, building like those layers and layers of snow during the Thanksgiving storm of 1958.

We reveled in the competition for a place on the football team, the basketball team, the baseball team. There was no such thing as "participation trophies"—rewards were earned through hard work, practice, daily drills, and teamwork.

There were early mornings runs to become faster. There were afternoons spent playing shirts and skins pickup games in vacant lots. Practice, practice, practice. Each day took a little time and a little more effort. Nothing was a given, everything was earned, and then we tried to do even better.

Along with physical activity, there was school work, studies, homework. Grades were also earned, there was no other way. Books had to be read, multiplication tables had to be memorized, along with the dates from history and the rules of spelling and punctuation.

At the time, I didn't notice the foundation that was being laid; it was subtle and seemed a normal part of growing up. As an adult, I now see the value and importance of that foundation. I see in my own children how challenges require them to rise to the best of their abilities.

Slowly, like a tree, one ring at a time, those experiences helped to strengthen and shape my childhood, my teen years, my growth, maturity, and who I am. I became more and more aware of the reality of the country to which I was born. I came to understand that the health and the vitality of the nation are interconnected. I learned that to succeed you must build; to build, you must plan; to plan you must study. For someone to achieve, they must demand more from themselves.

From Detroit, Michigan, to Pittsburg, Pennsylvania, from High Point, North Carolina, to Dalton, Georgia, American towns grew and flourished around major industries. Mill towns and mining drove a growing and thriving economy. Jobs grew, unions organized and families moved into new homes.

Assembly lines throbbed as manufacturing support grew to feed the major industries. Steel was forged and hammered into railroad track and rebar. Stone and lime were mined and crushed at batch plants, mixed and poured by the millions of cubic yards into highways, bridges, and tunnels. Many more tons of concrete supported huge high-rise buildings and factories. The World Trade Center, once such a prominent part of New York City, was built using steel forged four states away and in my hometown.

Housing developments grew across the landscape. New homes were built at a rate never before seen anywhere in the world. Investors put their own money on the line to underwrite the initial cost of projects large and small.

In these towns, many opened their first savings account at the community bank. The dimes and dollars in those savings accounts added up. Residents used that money to better their lives and the lives of their families. Banks underwrote more mortgages; more homes were built, and people secured pride of home-ownership. Banks made prudent investments in solid projects; the economy grew, factories were built and then expanded; jobs were available for anyone willing to work. People set even more money aside in those accounts with an eye toward the day when their children would go to college, a day when they would build a vacation home, a time when they would retire.

Among those hard-working families was Mr. & Mrs. Thomas Falter, my parents. They were merchants and service providers, Their business was hair salons and selling beauty products, it is a noble profession, and they were well respected in the town. My parents were admired for their dedication to hard work and their personal ethics. The American dream wove its way through every aspect of their lives.

After many years serving the community and their family with their chosen profession, the opportunity presented itself for my father to join Prudential Insurance, and a new chapter opened in our lives. Dad was one of those guys who made friends easily. He was quick to smile, engage in conversation, or extend a helping hand. He was a listener, and he was a doer.

He was most known for having a good heart and a desire to help others, this all made Dad a natural when he put down his sheers and moved into life insurance. People know when someone is genuine and involved, and whether or not they care. My dad's focus was always on clients' needs. In those days, there were no 401(k) plans. There was no financial planning for Mr. & Mrs. Blue Collar. Americans thought their home ownership and savings would be enough to carry them through their sunset years.

Many people went from high school into their first job, worked hard and perhaps moved to a new position after a few years. They bought a house, raised a family and saved a few dollars each week. Social Security and even U.S. Savings Bonds were the basis for most retirement plans, in the best of cases, supplemented by a vested pension.

Within a few years of becoming a Prudential agent, Dad was doing well enough to move to Florida. We left the cold of the West Virginia panhandle behind, moving to a larger home on Overcash Drive in Dunedin, Florida. Our new home was located just a few short blocks from the beaches of the gulf coast, and close to the stadium where Major League Baseball teams held their spring training.

I was a young teenager, enjoying the sunshine and tropical weather after the snow and long winters of Weirton. I was in heaven. My new school friends were talented and hard-working, with strong study habits and good grades. I started my first humble business venture, mowing lawns and doing landscaping throughout the neighborhood.

Although we were living in a more affluent neighborhood, the same forces that shaped my vision of America growing up in West Virginia were evident. American cars lined the streets, American furniture made our homes comfortable and welcoming. American steel and concrete built the roads and bridges; even the barrel tile on our roof was locally made.

Families budgeted for the future, made deposits each pay period into those small local banks and bought life insurance from agents like my Dad whom they trusted and relied upon for wise financial advice. Seeing these neighbors interact with my Dad was my introduction to the reality that men like my father were instrumental in helping families plan for the challenges to come.

CHAPTER 2

Co-Pilot for Life

After a few years in Florida, the large number of clients my father had gathered back home in Weirton, West Virginia, required his attention and return to the upper panhandle. In those days, each agent was responsible for following his "book" of clients to ensure ongoing coverage and payment. That personal touch was part of my father's success, a small lesson I, his youngest son, haven't forgotten.

When it came time to choose a place to further my education, I decided on MidAmerica Nazarene University, in part because I felt the people there shared a common value and belief systems. The university in Olathe, Kansas, fit my demeanor, as it represented strong core principles and was cost-effective. I understood that a conservative approach to my life was rewarding and fulfilling.

At school and social gatherings, I was active, but generally considered to be quiet and a bit shy. I studied hard, applied myself, tried to absorb as much knowledge and information as possible.

I had been spending time with a lovely young lady, enjoying the benefits of college life and activities, but we both knew that we never would be more than good friends. Sensing this, she introduced me to one of her best friends, and the magic began. I looked up from my books, I heard this magical laugh, and my life changed forever.

In front of me was a bright, bubbly, beautiful poster child for America. She was "the girl next door"—if you lived in a great neighborhood. Smart and sensitive, caring and outgoing, endowed with empathy and a sharp wit, I had found the love of my life, the future mother of my children, the life partner I have since come to rely upon every single day.

Amy Karcher was on her way to a degree in education, following her love for children into a career path that was not known to be financially rewarding but which gave her a sense of purpose and accomplishment. She was determined to become a teacher, devoted to the future students whose minds she would open to the world around them. She would graduate and go on to become that special teacher students remember years after they leave school and venture into the world. She was gifted to teach and direct, always with a kind heart and gentle enlightened wisdom.

Watching Amy with a class full of first-graders gave me a delightful vision into our future together, when this scene would play out with our own children. It was one of the many facets of this precious diamond that showed me what our future together would bring.

Our trail to a life together was not without its big decisions. At the end of our freshman year, I was offered the opportunity to work with my father in the insurance industry. Now logistics really became important.

Dad had returned to his core insurance business in Weirton, West Virginia. He was maintaining and enforcing his practice in our hometown, even as the industry was changing and expanding. He was working day and night, always available to his clients, always willing to make time to listen to each one. He needed someone he could rely upon to treat his clients with that same care and respect.

This was an opportunity for me to learn from a man I trusted and admired, a man who listened to his clients and a man who respected everyone he met. My father would be my mentor; he would share with me the values and lessons hard learned through his own career.

Joining my father in his practice came with its own special circumstances, not the least of which was geographic location.

Both Florida and West Virginia were fertile fields for this type of business, with a constant flow of income, activity, and referrals from existing clients. Our client base was expanding, I was learning a new career from one of the best in the industry, but I too would be splitting my time between doing business in Weirton, West Virginia, and attending college in Olathe, Kansas.

The key consideration was that when I was working in West Virginia, Amy was a thousand miles away in middle Kansas, and that was where my heart was leading me. I believe my father saw the reality of the growing relationship between myself and Amy. He knew that Amy was a very special woman and that spending our lives together was the best possible outcome for our future.

My father not only took me into his end of the business and tutored me, but he also helped me to relocate to Kansas to be close to Amy. Dad went as far as to help organize and launch the business in Kansas, and when the time came, he was wise and caring enough to encourage me to explore moving on and hang my licenses at another agency.

By his actions, my father showed me the hard choices that were the right choices. I learned that doing the right thing for others was really the only choice a man of honor should ever make. It is one of the priceless lessons from a man with a big heart.

As I applied the lessons learned from my father, I became more comfortable and more productive. I was refining my presentations, learning to focus on my clients' needs, anticipating their questions. At age nineteen, I received my first recognition from the insurance industry.

As Amy and I started to plan for that future, we were spending long hours talking and sharing our hopes and dreams. With a matched pair of rings, inscribed 1st Corinthians, 13:7 ("Love bears all things, believes all things, hopes all things, endures all things"), we stood before God and family and became Mr. & Mrs. Mark Falter. We have never looked back.

Like most newlywed couples, we had to budget carefully, watching our pennies, we drove a road-weary, but American-made Chevy Cavalier, we lived in a small apartment complex in Shawnee, Kansas. Cozy and cost-effective as that one-bedroom, one-bath apartment was, it quickly became the center of our universe.

CHAPTER 3

Listening and Learning

Like most newlyweds, Amy and I were on an unimaginably tight budget, watching pennies and learning how to stretch dimes and quarters. Date nights were not about spending money we did not have at a fancy restaurant, they were about spending time together. We took long walks, we talked and dreamed and we sat in our tiny living room and watched a movie on television. Best of all, we were building a relationship of trust and shared understanding.

We were balancing the demands of a young couple, a new marriage, and two new careers. Both of us learning and applying new talents and abilities which take the deft footwork of an Olympic figure skater, hitting the ice for the very first time.

I learned that Amy has this amazing ability to look at the tornado of daily life and triage all the looming crisis and brush fires, without losing sight of the joys and blessings. Class sizes in those days were twenty-four to twenty-six children, and Amy embraced each child as her own. She would spend late evenings reviewing how each child faced the day, preparing lesson plans, and most importantly, recognizing the needs of every student entrusted to her.

In an educational culture of "teaching to the test" and passing students on just to meet the quota, Amy was that teacher who students will recall fondly decades after graduation. Watching

Amy as she worked at our kitchen table, listening as she recounted the day's events from the classroom, affirmed my confidence in the decision to spend my life with this very special lady.

Along with learning and perfecting our career abilities, it was important that Amy and I, individually and as a couple, embrace fiscal responsibility. It is not enough to simply spend less money; it is critical to get the best value for the money spent.

I drove a sensible American car, a Chevrolet Cavalier, simple and easy to maintain. Routine oil changes rotating the tires and paying attention to small problems before they became big problems. It was my daily driver for several years, and it represented a realistic return on investment.

To meet the same challenge, we bought a basic Honda for Amy, which she drove every day for the next twenty-one years. Not only did that little Honda take Amy to and from work, but it also brought our three children home from the hospital as each was born. It took them to school and church; it took us on family nights out, it took us on day trips and vacations. Year in and year out, that slightly more expensive choice returned more value per dollar and justified our choice.

And, sixteen years after we bought it, as our first-born, Ashley, learned to drive and earned her driver's license, we passed the little car along to her for her first car. A few years later, Ashley was able to hand the keys off to her younger brother, Caleb, when his time came, and then a few years after that, Caleb passed the keys to Joshua.

Amy and I learned quickly that we had to outline a realistic budget and stick to it in order to ensure a secure future for our family. We had to maintain strict control over our spending, and we had to make choices about instant gratification being less important than long-term security.

I would get in our Cavalier, and add a few hundred more miles each day, calling on clients, learning the routine and the rhythm of the insurance industry. My average day was ten hours or more of direct interaction with clients, and hours of research and analysis to provide the correct insurance option for their needs.

There is no "one-size-fits-all" insurance product for every single client. Each client, each family, each situation is different. That was one of the very first lessons learned from my father, and it was a large reason for his personal success. My father knew that the farmer with 2,000 acres and 500 cattle needed different coverage than the soon to be retiring mill worker who had paid off the mortgage on his small home and hoped to leave enough for his grandchildren to go to college.

Just as I treasure the relationship I share with my Amy, my children, my grandchild, so too do I treasure my relationship with my clients. Their success is the measure of my success. All of my drive and determination is wasted if I don't give my very best efforts to each and every client.

As my career grew and the number of clients kept increasing, I studied the relationships that were building and looked for the commonalities of my most satisfying, and successful, client interactions. I was looking for patterns of success and analyzing the factors that my clients most appreciated.

As it turned out, the most consistent element, the single thing that was repeated over and over again was always the same. That consistent comment from satisfied and successful client relationships has always been, "Mark always takes the time to listen to me."

From the moment a client walks in the door of our office, we begin the process of learning all we can about what their most important objectives and motivations might be. A member of our team greets them warmly, shows them the basic information about our firm, and answers their preliminary questions. We begin to assess their personality traits and their comfort level, all with an eye toward giving them the very best service we have to offer.

When I sit down with a client in my office for a "one on one" first meeting, I am not sitting behind some large, designer-inspired executive desk; I am seated with them at a roundtable, to ensure that they feel comfortable to speak freely and openly.

I do not want my clients to be awed by a fancy office; I want them to be frank and relaxed.

Many people begin interviews, and relationships, with chatter and unrelated conversations—but I try to focus on gathering, and sharing, as much information as, possible. We call this focus "N.S.T." (No Small Talk)—not because there is no conversation, but because every conversation, every communication, and every word a client shares with me is not "Small Talk"—it is all "Real Talk."

One large wall of my office is a whiteboard where I can write and diagram the important factors the client reveal to me. I can show, in real time, in simple diagrams and basic charts the factors which will affect the client's future. On my desk is a pad and pencil, similarly useful in presenting information in a plain, easy to understand format.

A client who has become a close personal friend is a retiree from John Deere. As he tells it, when he was meeting with other advisors, they overwhelmed him with stacks of computer printouts and "Monte Carlo simulations," all of which left him more confused than when he walked in the door. They showed him plug-and-play portfolio programs and standardized formulas they, or their firms, already had on hand, and which gave them a comfort level. He did not feel he and his family were the most important part of the equation.

When he and I sat down, I showed him in black and white, based on his particular circumstances, the unique steps I recommended to ensure his comfortable retirement. We discussed the tax planning that was most favorable for his circumstances. Most importantly, I listened as he described the amount of income he felt he needed in retirement.

I did not give him reams and reams of babble-speak, I drew a few quick scenarios on the whiteboard, and I talked to him like the friends we have become, always answering his questions in a form and manner he understood, and which was comfortable for him.

In exchange, he shared with me the goals he had in mind. He told me what his needs were going into the future, how he wanted to spend his retirement years, what level of risk he found acceptable. With this information, I came to a greater understanding of how I could best help him. I doubt we could have reached this level of mutual understanding if we simply focused on computer programs spitting out formulaic "one-size-fits-all" advice.

Each and every single one of my clients deserves the same attention to their needs and to their specific situation. They also deserve to be treated with respect, honesty, and understanding; I believe we do this to the best of our ability, each and every day.

Every client has a different personality, a different threshold of risk, a different temperament and a different "temperature"; it is my job to assess each of those factors and present viable answers. More than any other motivation, helping clients to identify problems, create solutions, and plan for their future is the focus of my career.

CHAPTER 4

Charting Your Course

People don't plan to fail, they fail to plan. Many people are taught how to make money in school but not what to do with it once they've made it. A recent study showed 22 percent of Americans have $5,000 or less saved for retirement, and 15 percent have saved nothing at all.[1] Without a written blueprint, you could end up there, too.

However, in the end, it's not just about how much money you amass, it's the income you receive from that money that is important. For this, planning is paramount.

At MidAmerican Wealth Advisory Group, we believe our planning process is different. We take you through a step-by-step, understandable process to develop a plan that is tailored to you and your needs. It's not just a one-size-fits-all, cookie-cutter approach.

We consider planning for expenses and emergencies a "Murphy Repellent," meaning we want Murphy (of Murphy's Law) to bypass you and go to someone else's door who is not prepared.

Financial professionals, such as ourselves, can help someone create this strategy by asking questions you may not know how to answer yet. You don't know what you don't know!

---

[1] Donna Fuscaldo. Investopedia. August 16, 2021. "Retirement Without Savings?" https://www.investopedia.com/articles/personal-finance/111815/what-retirement-will-look-without-savings.asp

We get to know you as a person: your wants, needs, and goals. We ask questions and let you answer; we don't come to a meeting with preconceived or packaged questions and tell you what we think you need. We want to really get to know you as a person and your temperament. Many advisors find out your temperament when the market goes down; we want to find out long before that, and that can't be done with a prepackaged temperament quiz.

Planning and building a safe and secure future with one of my clients is similar to building a custom home for a family. Anyone can go online and pick a stock blueprint package for a house, but it is the specific needs of your family that make a house a home for you and your family.

Before you can design the roof, you must know the size of the house. You must have a concept of the needs of the people who will live in the house. Will this be a starter home for a young couple? Will this be home to a middle-aged couple with teenagers, or to empty nesters with children in college? Will this be a home for an older couple still working, staying socially active, and hosting large parties, with grandchildren who come to visit and stay overnight? Will this be the retirement home for a couple with some health issues or special needs?

Each stage of life and circumstance requires a different design and different planning. The young couple just starting out might want a small home in a trendy neighborhood hoping for a future resale at a profit. They might want to put a greater part of their income into savings for a larger home in the future.

The slightly older couple with children in school might need a home with four bedrooms, a bath for each child, and a modest mortgage so they can put more money into college funds for those children.

Once those children are off to college or starting families of their own, the same couple might want a home where they can entertain, or on a golf course or country club. They might feel comfortable knowing that their mortgage payments will be part of an equity investment for their retirement.

They might want a second home to use for vacations, for rental income, or a place to eventually retire. They are thinking about the savings and investments they will need to carry them through their retirement years.

Having reached retirement age, that same couple might have sold that big six-bedroom house in the country club neighborhood and may want to take the proceeds of that sale to build a small house in which they will spend the rest of their lives.

Once an architect has met with a client and has discussed the overall needs, wants, and preferences that client has shared, far more work must be done if the plans on paper are to be transferred into reality.

An architect must consider the variables of the site plan, soil composition, the slope of the building site, the location of utilities, access roads, and even how to get materials to the job site. The responsibility also includes cost estimates, assessing the practicality of the project, knowing the rules and regulations of the building code, the zoning, land use density and more.

Above all, the architect must always consider the needs of the client. They must do everything in their power to keep the client safe from making a bad choice, building on unstable ground, even spending more than they can afford on extras, revisions, and changing the plans in the middle of construction.

In each stage of life, the quest for a safe and comfortable home remains the same, but the specifics of what meets those needs change. The architect who just collects a fee and pulls a pre-made set of plans off the shelf does the client no service. The architect who takes the time to listen to the client, who learns the important facts about their stage of life, who carefully considers their financial options before designing a house has a far better chance of meeting the needs of their family.

Just as the home you want for your family must be well-designed, cost-effective, and practical, so too must your financial planning for your family be well-designed, cost-effective, and practical. Like the architect working to put a roof over your family, a dedicated financial advisor works to put a sheltering roof over the funds you have worked so hard to accumulate. In both cases, without a solid, well-planned, well-structured foundation, the end results could be unsafe and unsatisfactory.

In the pages that follow, I'll discuss some of the strategies used in our firm to help provide a foundation for your retirement and financial confidence for years to come. But first, let's take a look at some of the common roadblocks that can impede your path to a dream retirement.

Potential Risks to Your Ideal Retirement

Ever feel like life gets in the way and prevents you from doing things you should not ignore? I think if we're honest with ourselves, we've all put off obligations we know are important.

In your case, you may be reading this book because it's time to get serious about financial planning and, specifically, devising a way to best prepare for retirement. A retirement income plan should be based on more components than just your investments or your finances. The preparation of that strategy begins with your desires, ambitions, and goals for this fulfilling season of life.

There's no such thing as a silly question. Not when one of the most common questions we hear from folks regarding retirement is, "Am I going to be okay?" Often, it seems, people are reluctant to meet with financial professionals because they worry they might sound uneducated. Yet, it's understandable for you to be a novice when it comes to financial issues and retirement concerns. You've been busy with your lives and your careers. Time spent away from work has meant time spent being around those you love and engaging in the activities you enjoy. Retirement provides the opportunity to do even more of that, while not fretting over work obligations.

Concerns people have about what they may encounter during retirement can be far-reaching and still perfectly legitimate. For a quick snapshot, I want to provide a brief sampling of wide-ranging issues that can come up during discussions about what to potentially brace for in retirement. This book will touch on many of these issues in further detail.

Politics: A presidential election often stirs emotions regarding potential effects on the economy. Investors grow anxious about how a new president can influence market returns. It's Congress, however, that establishes tax laws and passes spending bills. Yet the president can indirectly affect the economy and the stock market in various ways such as the appointment of policymakers, development of international relations, and influential sway on new legislation.

Taxes: An example of a president's influence can be cited in signature legislation passed during Donald Trump's presidency, the Tax Cuts and Jobs Act of 2017. However, our tax system remains progressive, so the more you earn, the higher the tax rate within each tax bracket of subsequently higher income. A thorough understanding of tax regulations can be crucial. A financial professional can help identify potential issues a tax professional can help solve.

Inflation: Government spending, which most recently spiked with relief packages designed to assist U.S. citizens during the COVID-19 pandemic, can fuel concerns of inflationary hikes stemming from an influx of money thrust at the same consumer goods. A retiree's income can be impacted by the effect inflation can have on a fixed budget. The value of currency decreases because inflation erodes purchasing power.

Health pandemic: The coronavirus outbreak could impact how Americans view risks and re-examine healthy habits. That, potentially, could be one of the effects of COVID-19 as we assess how long a pandemic can last and if others will occur in our lifetimes. The cost of health care can be surprising throughout retirement. It could become an issue people focus on even more following the pandemic, which had a particularly acute impact on some U.S. elder care facilities.

Cybersecurity: Think you'll give up your smartphone in retirement? No way, right? It's here to stay, along with other intellectual gadgetry, including devices that have not been patented or invented. Retirees are becoming more tech-savvy, yet they can also be more trusting, which can be problematic when responding to potential scammers by phone, text, or email. Cybercrime often uses technology to target potential victims. Scammers, much like technology, figure to only grow more sophisticated over time.

CHAPTER 5

Cleared for Takeoff

Ground school is the first step in the process of earning a Federal Aviation Agency Pilot license. A private pilot's license is required before moving on to all other classifications. It is at ground school that the basic laws of aerodynamics are studied, taught, learned, and tested. Pilots must have a basic understanding of the physical laws which allow something heavier than air to leave the ground, and to return, hopefully at a controlled rate and to a predetermined location, under the direction of the pilot in command.

No aircraft, of any type or description, is exempt from the four basic components of the flight equation: lift/weight and thrust/drag. Hot air balloon or rocketship to the space station, those four measurements must be taken into account.

Lift is the ability to rise relative to the surrounding air. It is the end result of the difference between areas of different air pressure.

Weight is the load which must be gotten airborne. It is the force of gravity acting in a downward direction, toward the very center of the earth.

Thrust is the forward motion and rate of that motion. It is created by the engines of the aircraft.

Drag is the combination of factors which negatively affect the flight. Drag is anything which slows the passage of the aircraft in a forward direction.

In the case of an airplane in flight, it's always a balancing act with four different forces. For the plane to take flight, thrust must exceed drag or friction, and lift must be greater than the weight of the plane. For landing, thrust is reduced to less than drag, and lift must be less than weight.

Think of your investment funds in the same terms, and you get the following interchangeable forces:

Lift: The upward movement in the price or market value of your investment. It is the rate at which the value of your investment improves, or it may be the interest rate earned on your investment.

Weight: The sum total value of the investment.

Thrust: The speed of the positive movement in the value of your investment.

Drag: Anything that reduces the forward motion (growth) of your investments. Management costs, commissions, and other fees are all "drag." And additional "drag" on your investment is "risk"—if the risk is greater than the reward, you certainly are not "getting off the ground.

Takeoff and landing are the two most dangerous times during any flight. During takeoff, the pilot aligns with the centerline of the runway, clears for surrounding traffic, and applies throttle or thrust. As the plane moves forward, the difference in air pressure above and below the wing creates lift. At the same time, the plane is moving forward, things like the friction of the tires on the runway, the antennas and pilot tubes, struts and other factors act to slow the forward progress of the plane down the runway that is "drag."

At some point, the lift is greater than the weight of the aircraft, and that's when it begins to rise.

Then there are speeds and rates of climb that become important. These are called "V" speeds.

Speed of normal operations: This is generally based upon a "standard rate of climb," typically 500 feet per minute (vertical rise). If your desired cruise altitude is 3,500 feet, and you take off from an airport located at 1,500 feet elevation, you have to climb 2,000 feet. At 500 feet per minute, it will take four minutes to reach your cruise altitude.

But suppose you want to reach that "cruise altitude" faster?

Best speed of climb: You can apply more power, go faster and increase the lift generated and you will reach that altitude in 3 minutes instead of 4 minutes, (make more frequent contributions to your plan.) The problem is that the available income opportunities for most people come at fixed intervals, where will you get more frequent paychecks?

Best angle of climb: You can change the angle of your flight, climbing at an even greater rate of climb, and reach that same cruise altitude in 2 minutes instead of 3 or 4, (make larger contributions to your plan.) Making larger contributions to your plan may result in a shortfall of available funds to meet your present needs. You will "stall" because you don't have sufficient funds left for current obligations.

Each change in your flight profile comes with an associated cost, it is important to understand the cost of those changes before they become too great to overcome.

So, what does this have to do with your investment portfolio?

It's the first of January, your new year's resolution is to begin an investment account, so you have to have a "field elevation" – a starting point. This is the amount of money you begin with, so let's assume that today is the very first day you begin to take action on your investment plan. You get paid each week, today is payday, and you have decided to put $125 in your investment account. Your current runway elevation is $0, and you put $125 under your mattress.

Next payday, you put another $125 under your mattress. Next payday you put yet another $125 under your mattress— and the last payday of the month another $125. In four weeks, you have $500 under your mattress, it looks like your "standard rate of climb" is $500 per month, $6,000 per year.

You intend to put $6,000 per year, every year, into your retirement account. That is your cruising altitude, the level that you want to maintain until you get to your destination or target fund.

Your friend Marvin calls and says he has a deal for you. He has a hand-raised Scarlet Macaw that needs a home, do you want to buy it for $100? Well, that is a deal, so you grab one of the pictures of Mr. Franklin under your mattress, and you head over to your friend Marvin. Beautiful bird, just what you wanted and home you go. Your rate of climb has just decreased to $400 per month. You can still reach your target altitude of $6,000 per year, but you will have to make up that $100 by making an additional deposit of $100 by working overtime for the next two weeks. Your Best Speed of Climb has changed because you're making payments more rapidly, just to keep up.

You get back to your apartment and rig up a free perch for your new parrot, and things go well all weekend long. Monday you leave for work and "Paco" the parrot is content on its perch. When you get home Monday night, Paco is nowhere to be found. As you search the apartment, you find Paco in the bathroom, where he has chewed the wood door frame to shreds.

After spending an hour on Craig's List, you grab another $100 bill from beneath the mattress, and you head to the store to buy a big cage for Paco. Your rate of climb has now dropped to $300 per month. You will still be able to reach your cruising altitude, but now you must deposit $200 per month for the next month in order to stay on track. Your Best Rate of Climb has now changed.

You put Paco in the new cage the next morning and head to work. An hour after you get to work you get a call from the police. Your neighbor heard a woman screaming in your apartment, they are on the scene and can hear her too; you need to come check it out.

Back to your apartment, you open the door, there is Paco in the cage, going through his repertoire of screams and whistles. You cover the cage and head back to your job at the Bedrock Computer Center. Your biggest client is walking out the door with the new computer he just bought from Elroy, and Elroy got the commission for the sale. That is going to hurt come payday.

On Friday, you cash your paycheck, (now minus the commission on the big computer sale) and head home. You put $200 under the mattress, and then you open the mail. It seems the apartment manager found out about the screaming parrot episode and is invoking the pet deposit rule. You need to add $100 to your rent payment today to cover the deposit.

After the $200 you put under the mattress to maintain your "rate of climb," the $100 pet deposit is going to leave you short for the week. No Starbucks "double soy, double foam espresso latte" for you this week. But you are at least on track to maintain your original planned normal rate of climb.

The following week, you faithfully put another two pictures of Mr. Franklin under the mattress. And you do it again the following week and the week after that. You have re-established your planned $500 per month rate of climb, but the flow chart looks like a roller coaster.

Now that you are back on your planned rate of climb, you put $125 under the mattress each week for another month. It is now three months into your plan, and there are $1,500 under your mattress. You're on course, right where you wanted to be. Then your car breaks down. $1,000 later, your Hyundai has a new timing belt, and you are back on the road. There are now only $500 under the mattress, and you are way below your planned rate of climb.

Back and forth it goes, up one week, add another picture of Mr. Franklin, down next week, two pictures of Mr. Franklin go for a walk. As hard as you try, it seems that every month there is an unexpected expense that drains that small stack of Benjamins under your mattress and your rate of climb is never "normal."

On the first of June, you are halfway through the year, and you receive a certified letter from the apartment complex management company. There have been so many complaints about your parrot that they are canceling your lease and you have to move. You have thirty days to vacate.

As you start looking for another apartment, you find one that is closer to work, has a community swimming pool but is $500 per month more than you are currently paying. You like the apartment, but they have a very firm no pets policy. You realize that no matter where you move, Paco the parrot will be a problem.

On the other hand, since he has been living with you, his feathers have filled out, and he has learned two dozen new words and phrases. You take some photos and put an ad in the BirdFinders.com online edition, and a guy from California wants to buy the parrot. You sell the bird for $3,000 and decide to put it all under the mattress. Once again, you are at the right rate of climb.

Congratulations, you have, to use a real estate term, just "flipped" the bird, and have found a nicer, but more expensive place to live.

You transformed a problem situation into a positive benefit. Your rate of climb has been all over the place, but overall, you're on track.

Except there's that additional $500 per month rent on the new apartment. This leaves you without any extra money to put under the mattress. You end the year with just $3,000 in your investment account, half of what you projected for the year.

At a New Year's Eve party at the new "Food Lovers" restaurant down in Florida, you meet a classmate you have not seen since high school. As you talk, she tells you she is planning to buy a sailboat in ten years and spend the winter sailing in the Carribean. She mentions she's already a third of the way to the amount she needs to be able to buy the boat. Her plan is to only work stateside during the hurricane season. She explains that she has been working with an advisor who helped her get organized and restructured her taxes and expenses. She suggests you talk to her "money guy" then hands you their card.

You make a new, New Year's resolution: you're going to call the guy and get some help.

On the 7th of January, you meet with the recommended advisor and review your options. Because you work on commission, he suggests a formula for payroll deductions that is a little less each week, but which automatically adds your quarterly bonus to the account. Your advisor also suggests some changes in your tax planning and insists you put your funds into a 401(k) so you cannot access it every time there is a short-term event. Instead of depositing $125 each week, you are now depositing $100 each week, and you have enough to pay down your credit card bills a little at a time.

You decide to stop sleeping with $3,000 under your mattress and put them into an account, with automatic reinvestment of interest. Not only are you less inclined to use that money that you'll need later in life, but it can now compound as it's reinvested.

Since you never even see Mr. Franklin each week, you no longer have to put him under the mattress yourself, it is put someplace with more promise before you get your paycheck. Even better, since Mr. Franklin is no longer easy to access and be taken from under the mattress, you stop thinking of those funds as "available."

Another year goes by. You have more problems with that darn Hyundai, but because you have paid off the previous outstanding balance on your credit card, you can use that card and pay for the repairs over a four-month period and stay within your budget.

At the end of the year, when you get your account, you look at the numbers. You started the year with $3,000. You put $400 per month into the account via automatic payroll deduction, and that adds $4,800 to the original amount. Although you expected a balance of $7,800, you're pleasantly surprised to find that your account is actually higher.

You had also decided to have quarterly bonus checks auto-deposited paid into your account, that has added another $2,500 to your investment funds.

With your interest reinvested, you gained another $137.36.

The plan has your employer match your contributions to the investment account up to a certain percent of your salary, so you have an extra $1,200 in the investment account as well.

In one year, instead of putting $6,000 into your investment account, you have actually added $8,637.36—and you have done it on $400 per month instead of $500 per month.

With the changes the advisor suggested, you now have a total of $11,637.36 in your investment account. Remember, you actually put $25 per week less into the account, but you did it every single week. You never drew any money out, you put any bonus money into the account before you could spend it, and you are getting a tax refund.

You have smoothed out the rate of climb to a steady trajectory, and have avoided the whipsaw up and down swings. And best of all, you have met your annual goal.

It is always best to have a flight plan filed before leaving the airport, but if you have to make a course correction in route, it is better to do it as soon as possible before you are miles off course.

So, you fly along year after year at your previous "cruise altitude," and the total in your investment fund gets larger and larger each year. Thankfully, you are also doing even better in your job, as advancements and raises come your way, you meet with your advisor each year on taxes and you also discuss options on putting money away for retirement that go above and beyond 401(k) options. Now you're picking up speed and your not only getting to your destination, but you're also getting there faster.

By the fifth year, you are actually putting money into your investment accounts at twice the original rate, and the account is generating more and more income each year.

Congratulations. Between "flipping the bird" your first year and prudent planning the next nine years, you have increased your average contribution, you have advantaged those funds, and you have advanced toward your goals at a faster rate than you anticipated.

By the tenth year at cruising altitude, you are ahead of schedule, and you start thinking about buying a sailboat yourself and sailing the islands of the Caribbean each winter. Now is when you find out that the other most dangerous time of a flight is the descent and landing.

When a pilot has the destination airport in sight, he changes the power settings; he throttles back, trims the aircraft for a controlled descent at a standard rate, again usually 500 feet per minute. One of the most important gauges on his instrument panel is the altimeter; it displays not only the altitude at which the plane is flying but also the rate of inclination or descent.

It is important to have a good idea of how close to the airport you are, as well as the difference between your current altitude and the field elevation. You plan to set up a standard rate of descent of 500 feet per minute and to stay on the glideslope all the way to the runway.

You start "withdrawing altitude" in the form of the disbursements from your investment funds to your household accounts. If you make equal withdraws each month, you should have enough to last you until you are 104 years old before your funds are gone.

But what happens if you start drawing down those invested funds in larger amounts than planned? If $500 per month will last you thirty-four years until you are 104, what happens if you draw down $1,000 per month? Your funds will only last seventeen years. You must plan on dying no later than age eighty-seven or you will run out of funds before you run out of life.

If you do live to be 104, and you have drawn down your complete investment fund by age eighty-seven, on what will you live for those last seventeen years?

The ups and downs of dollar-cost averaging (DCA) and reverse dollar-cost averaging (RDCA) can have complex implications beyond just the food on your table and your anticipated personal expiration date. In many cases, you will be withdrawing funds based on required minimum distributions (RMD), and there will be specific tax liabilities as well.

Just as pilots rely upon the air traffic controller to monitor their departure time, take off, climb to altitude, path to destination/time to destination, approach and descent rates, touch down and shut down at the hanger, it is important that you, as the "pilot in command" of your own financial plane, have clear lines of communication with the control tower.

CHAPTER 6

Market Volatility

No part of your financial journey introduces more possibilities for ups and downs than the stock market. The potential for higher returns is counter-balanced by a higher level of risk and volatility.

Still, financial strategies tend to revolve around market-based products, for good reasons. For one thing, there is no other financial class that packs the same potential for growth, pound for pound, as stock-based products. Because of growth potential, inflation protection, and new opportunities, it may be unwise to avoid the market entirely.

However, along with the potential for growth is the potential for loss. At the time this book was written, many of the people I've seen in my office came in feeling uneasy because of the economic fallout of the COVID-19 outbreak of 2020, followed by the economic downturn, and the inflation spike that happened in 2022.

So how do we balance these factors? How do we try to satisfy both the need for protection and the need for growth?

For one thing, it is important to recognize the value of diversity. Now, I'm not just talking about the diversity of assets among different kinds of stocks, or even different kinds of stocks and bonds. That's only one kind of diversity; while important, both stocks and bonds, though different, are both still market-based products. Most market-based products, even within a diverse portfolio, tend to rise or lower as a whole, just like an incoming tide. Therefore, a portfolio diverse in only market-sourced products won't automatically protect your assets during times when the market declines.

In addition to the sort of "horizontal diversity" you have by purchasing a variety of stocks and bonds from different companies, I also suggest you think about "vertical diversity," or diversity among asset classes. This means having different product types, including securities products, bank products, and insurance products—with varying levels of growth potential, liquidity, and protection—all in accordance with your unique situation, goals, and needs.

I ask questions, and I don't just tell a person what they need. I have a reallocation meeting process where the client literally tells me how much of their money they want to keep in a stable form of investment. I don't come in with preconceived ideas and tell a person what they want. I also don't use our industry's standard tests to determine risk. To truly find out what a client's needs and desires are, I believe you must dig deeper and ask questions.

The Color of Money

When you're looking at the overall diversity of your portfolio, part of the equation is knowing which products fit in what category: what has liquidity, what has protection, and what has growth potential.

Before we dive in, keep in mind these aren't absolutes. You might think of liquidity, growth, and protection as primary colors. While some products will look pretty much yellow, red, or blue, others will have a mix of characteristics, making them more green, orange, or purple.

Growth

I like to think of the growth category as red. It's powerful, it's somewhat volatile, and it's also the category where we have the greatest opportunities for growth and loss. Often, products in the growth category will have a good deal of liquidity but very little protection. These are our market-based products and strategies, and we think of them mostly in shades of red and orange, to designate their growth and liquidity. Examples of "red" products include:

- Stocks
- Equities
- Exchange-traded funds
- Mutual funds
- Corporate bonds
- Real estate investment trusts
- Speculations
- Alternative investments

Liquidity

Yellow is my liquid category color. I typically recommend having at least enough yellow money to cover six months' to a year's worth of expenses in case of emergency. Yellow assets don't need a lot of growth potential; they just need to be readily available when we need them. The "yellow" category includes assets like:

- Cash
- Money market accounts

Protection

The color of protection, to me, is blue. Tranquil, peaceful, sure, even if it lacks a certain amount of flash. This is the direction I like to see people generally move toward as they're nearing retirement. The red, flashy look of stock market returns and the risk of possible overnight losses is less attractive as we near retirement and look for more consistency and reliability. While this category doesn't come with a lot of liquidity, the products here are backed by an insurance company, a bank, or a government entity. "Blue" products include things such as:

- Certificates of deposit (backed by banks)
- Government-based bonds (backed by the U.S. government)
- Life insurance (backed by insurance companies)
- Annuities (backed by insurance companies)

In our reallocation process, after a person has become a client of the firm, they tell us how much of their money they want in the market. We don't come to them with a pre-packaged plan. Once the allocation has been determined, we emphasize the need to stay the course, rather than selling and locking in losses when the market drops.

401(k)s

Since the decline of defined benefit plans (pensions) and the increased use of defined contribution plans, workplace 401(k)s and IRAs have become the primary retirement savings vehicle for many people. One of the biggest benefits is convenience. An employer can deposit money from your payroll directly into the 401(k) without you even lifting a finger. Best of all, many companies will match a certain percentage of your contributions. In many cases, this money grows tax-free until you take withdrawals.

However, it is important to be aware of how exactly the taxes work on your individual retirement accounts. Some IRAs, 401(k)s, 403(b)s, etc. are what I call "tax wrappers." What do I mean by that? Well, depending on your plan provider, a 401(k) could include target-date funds, passively managed products, stocks, bonds, mutual funds, or even variable, fixed, and fixed index annuities, all collected in one place and governed by rules (a.k.a. the "tax wrapper"). These rules govern how much money you can put inside, what ways you can put it in, when you will pay taxes on it, and when you can take the money out. Inside the 401(k), each of the products inside the "tax wrapper" might have its own fees or commissions, in addition to the management fee you pay on the 401(k) itself.

Now, fees can be troublesome. You can't get something for nothing, and fees are how many financial companies and professionals make a living. Yet, it's important to recognize even a fee with a fraction of a percentage point is money out of your pocket—money that represents not just the one-time fee of today but also represents an opportunity cost. A $100,000 IRA that earns 6 percent over a twenty-five-year period without investment fees would earn $430,000. But if just a 0.5 percent fee got factored into that investment, the IRA would be worth $379,000 in twenty-five years, a $50,500 decrease.[2] For someone close to retirement, how much do you think fees may have cost over their lifetime?

Even for those close to retirement, it's important to look at management fees and assess if you think you're getting what you pay for. Over the course of ten years, those costs can add up, and you may have decades ahead of you in which you will need to rely on your assets.

Dollar-Cost Averaging

With 401(k)s and other market-based retirement products, dollar-cost averaging is a concept that can work in your favor when you are investing for the long term. When the market is trending up, if you are consistently paying in money, month over month, great; your investments can grow, and you are adding to your assets. When the market takes a dip, no problem; your dollars buy more shares at a lower price. At some point, we hope the market will rebound, in which case your shares can grow and possibly be more valuable than they were before. This concept is what we call "dollar-cost averaging." While it can't ensure a profit or guarantee against losses, it's a time-tested strategy for investing in a volatile market.

---

[2] Pam Krueger. Kiplinger.com. January 8, 2021. "How to Spot (and Squash) Nasty Fees That Hide in Your Investments" https://www.kiplinger.com/retirement/retirement-planning/602043/how-to-spot-and-squash-nasty-fees-that-hide-in-your

However, when you are in retirement, this strategy may work against you. You may have heard of "reverse" dollar-cost averaging. Before, when the market lost ground, you were "buying at lower prices"; your dollars purchased more assets at a reduced price. Often when you are in retirement, you are no longer the purchaser; you are selling. So, in a down market, you have to sell more assets to make the same amount of money as what you made in a favorable market.

I've had lots of people step into my office to talk to me about this, emphasizing, "my advisor says the market always bounces back, and I have to just hold on for the long term."

There's some basis for this thinking; thus far, the market has always rebounded to higher heights than before. But this is no guarantee, and the prospect of potentially higher returns in five years may not be very helpful in retirement if you are relying on the income from those returns to pay this month's electric bill, for example.

To help address market volatility, we have lots of client reviews. Things will happen that cause the market to go down. Also, we do planning where we derive income from a portfolio that focuses on stability whether the market is down or up.

Is There a "Perfect" Product?

To bring us back around to the discussion of protection, growth, and liquidity, the ideal product would be a "ten" in all three categories, right? Completely guaranteed, doubling in size every few years, and accessible whenever you want. Does such a product exist? Absolutely not.

Instead of running in circles looking for that perfect product, the silver bullet, the unicorn of financial strategies, it's more important to circle back to the concept of a balanced, asset-diverse portfolio.

This is why your interests may be best served when you work with a trusted financial professional who knows what various financial products can do and how to use them in your personal retirement strategy.

CHAPTER 7

Longevity

You would think the prospect of the grave would loom more frightening as we age, yet many retirees say their number one concern is actually running out of money in their twilight years.[3] This fear is, unfortunately, justified, in part, because of one significant factor: We're living longer.

According to the Social Security Administration, in 1950, the average life expectancy for a sixty-five-year-old man was seventy-eight, and the average for a sixty-five-year-old woman was eighty-one. In the 2022 Trustees Report issued by the SSA, those averages were eighty-three and eighty-five, respectively.[4]

The bottom line of many retirees' budget woes comes down to this: They just didn't plan to live so long. Now, when we are younger and in our working years, that's not something we necessarily see as a bad thing; don't some people fantasize about living forever or, at least, reaching the ripe old age of one hundred?

However, with a longer lifespan, as we near retirement, we face a few snags. Our resources are finite—we only have so much money to provide income—but our lifespans can be unpredictably long, perhaps longer than our resources allow.

---

[3] Liz Weston. nerdwallet.com. March 25, 2021. "Will You Really Run Out of Money in Retirement?"
https://www.nerdwallet.com/article/finance/will-you-really-run-out-of-money-in-retirement
[4] Social Security Administration. 2022 Trustees Report. "Actuarial Life Table." https://www.ssa.gov/oact/STATS/table4c6.html

Also, longer lives don't necessarily equate with healthier lives. The longer you live, the more money you will likely need to spend on health care, even excluding long-term care needs like nursing homes.

You will also run into inflation. If you don't plan to live another twenty-five years but end up doing so, inflation at an average 3 percent will approximately double the price of goods over that time period. Put a harsh twist on that and the buying power of a ninety-year-old will be half of what they possessed if they retired at sixty-five.[5] And this is before you count the expenses of any potential health care or long-term care needs.

Because we don't necessarily get to have our cake and eat it, too, our collective increased longevity hasn't necessarily increased the healthy years of our lives. Typically, our life-extending care most widely applies to the time in our lives where we will need more care in general. Think of common situations like a pacemaker at eighty-five, or cancer treatment at seventy-eight.

"Wow, Mark," I can hear you say. "Way to start with the good news first."

I know, I've painted a grim picture, but all I'm concerned about here is cost. It's hard to put a dollar sign on life, but that is essentially what we're talking about when discussing longevity and finances. Living longer isn't a bad thing; it just costs more, and one key to a sound retirement strategy is preparing for it in advance.

We were managing the assests of one our clients, who we'll call Roxie, and she had the foresight to look into long-term care planning. She passed away after three years in a nursing home, and thanks to her planning, she never had to touch her assets. Her son is now our client, and all of her assets stayed intact.

From age eighty-five to eighty-eight, Roxie was more socially active, with many visits from family and friends. She

---

5 Bob Sullivan, Benjamin Curry. Forbes. April 28, 2021. "Inflation And Retirement Investments: What You Need to Know."
https://www.forbes.com/advisor/retirement/inflation-retirement-investments

participated in more activities than she had in the seven years since her husband died. Her planning from decades earlier allowed her to pass on a legacy to her children when she passed away herself. The legacy she left behind can be measured both in dollar signs *and* in other intangible ways.

Living longer may be more expensive, but it can be so meaningful when you plan for your "just-in-cases."

Retiring Early

A key part of planning for retirement revolves around retirement income. After all, retirement is cutting the cord that tethers you to your employer—and your monthly check. However, that check often comes with many other benefits, particularly health care. Health care is often the thing that can unexpectedly put dreams for an early retirement on hold. Some employers offer health benefits to their retired workers, but that number has declined drastically over the past several decades. In 1988, among employers who offered health benefits to their workers, 66 percent offered health benefits to their retirees. That number has since diminished to 29 percent.[6]

So, with employer-offered retirement health benefits on the wane, this becomes a major point of concern for anyone who is looking to retire, particularly those who are looking to retire before age sixty-five, when they would become eligible for Medicare coverage. Fidelity estimates that the average retired couple at age sixty-five will need approximately $300,000 for medical expenses, not including long-term care.[7] Do you think it's likely that cost will decrease?

---

[6] Henry J. Kaiser Family Foundation. October 8, 2020. "2020 Employer Health Benefits Survey Section Eleven: Retiree Health Benefits." https://www.kff.org/report-section/ehbs-2020-section-11-retiree-health-benefits

[7] Fidelity Viewpoints. Fidelity. May 6, 2021. "How to Plan for Rising Health Care Costs." https://www.fidelity.com/viewpoints/personal-finance/plan-for-rising-health-care-costs

Even if you are working until age sixty-five or have plans to cover your health expenses until that point, I often have clients who incorrectly assume Medicare is their golden ticket to cover all expenses. That is simply not the case.

Retiring Later

Planning for a long life in retirement partly depends on when you retire. While many people end up retiring earlier than they anticipated—due to injuries, layoffs, family crises, and other unforeseen circumstances—continuing to work past age sixty (and even sixty-five) is still a viable option for others and can be an excellent way to help establish financial comfort in retirement.

There are many reasons for this. For one, you obviously still earn a paycheck and the benefits accompanying it. Medical coverage and beefing up your retirement accounts with further savings can be significant by themselves but continuing your income also should keep you from dipping into your retirement funds, further allowing them the opportunity to grow.

Additionally, for many workers, their nine-to-five job is more than just clocking in and out. Having a sense of purpose can keep us active physically, mentally, and socially. That kind of activity and level of engagement may also help stave off many of the health problems that plague retirees. Avoiding a sedentary life is one of the advantages of staying plugged into the workforce, if possible.

We worked with a man named Dick who left work early and didn't really have any hobbies to fill his newfound free time. His wife passed away three years before he did, and he essentially quit living when she died. He spent the last three years of his life being a burden on his kids. He lost mobility because he went into retirement with no hobbies or anything that got him out of the house.

Health Care

Take a second to reflect on your health care plan. Although working up to or even past age sixty-five would allow you to avoid a coverage gap between your working years and Medicare, that may not be an option for you. Even if it is, when you retire, you will need to make some decisions about what kind of insurance coverage you may need to supplement your Medicare. Are there any medical needs you have that may require coverage in addition to Medicare? Did your parents or grandparents have any inherited medical conditions you might consider using a special savings plan to cover?

These are all questions that are important to review with your financial professional so you can be sure you have enough money put aside for health care.

Long-Term Care

Longevity means the need for long-term care is statistically more likely to happen. If you intend to pass on a legacy, planning for long-term care is paramount, since most estimates project nearly 70 percent of Americans will need some type of it.[8] However, this may be one of the biggest, most stressful pieces of longevity planning I encounter in my work. For one thing, who wants to talk about the point in their lives when they may feel the most limited? Who wants to dwell on what will happen if they no longer can toilet, bathe, dress, or feed themselves?

I get it; this is a less-than-fun part of planning. But a little bit of preparation now can go a long way!

When it comes to your longevity, just like with your goals, one of the important things to do is sit and dream. It may not be the fun, road-trip-to-the-Grand-Canyon kind of dreaming,

---

[8] LongTermCare.gov. February 18, 2020. "How Much Care Will You Need?" https://acl.gov/ltc/basic-needs/how-much-care-will-you-need

but you can spend time envisioning how you want your twilight years to look.

For instance, if it is important for you to live in your home for as long as possible, who will provide for the day-to-day fixes and to-dos of housework if you become ill? Will you set aside money for a service, or do you have relatives or friends nearby whom you could comfortably allow to help you? Do you prefer in-home care over a nursing home or assisted living? This could be a good time to discuss the possibility of moving into a retirement community versus staying where you are or whether it's worth moving to another state and leaving relatives behind.

These are all important factors to discuss with your spouse and children, as *now* is the right time to address questions and concerns. For instance, is aging in place more important to one spouse than the other? Are the friends or relatives who live nearby emotionally, physically, and financially capable of helping you for a time if you face an illness?

Many families I meet with find these conversations very uncomfortable, particularly when children discuss nursing home care with their parents. A knee-jerk reaction for many is to promise they will care for their aging parents. This is noble and well-intentioned, but there needs to be an element of realism here. Does "help" from an adult child mean they stop by and help you with laundry, cooking, home maintenance, and bills? Or does it mean they move you into their spare room when you have hip surgery? Are they prepared to help you use the restroom and bathe if that becomes difficult for you to do on your own?

I don't mean to discourage families from caring for their own; this can be a profoundly admirable relationship when it works out. However, I've seen families put off planning for late-in-life care based on a tenuous promise that the adult children would care for their parents, only to watch as the support system crumbles. Sometimes this is because the assumed caregiver hasn't given serious thought to the preparation they would need, both in a formal sense and regarding their personal physical, emotional, and financial commitments. This is often also because we can't see the future: Alzheimer's disease and other maladies of old age can exact a heavy toll. When a loved one reaches the point where he or she is at risk of wandering away or needs help with two or more activities of daily living, it can be more than one person or family can realistically handle.

If you know what you want, communicate with your family about both the best-case and worst-case scenarios. Then, hope for the best, and plan for the worst.

Realistic Cost of Care

Wrapped up in your planning should be a consideration for the cost of long-term care. One study estimates that by 2030, the nation's long-term care costs could reach $2.5 trillion as roughly 24 million Americans require some type of long-term care.[9] The potential costs for such care and treatment can be underestimated, especially by those who have maintained robust health and find it difficult to envision future declines to their condition.

Another piece of planning for long-term care costs is anticipating inflation. It's common knowledge that prices have been and keep rising, which will lower your purchasing power on everything from food to medical care. Long-term care is a big piece of the inflation-disparity pie, which is part of why many find their estimates of nursing home care widely miss the mark. According to one survey, people expected to pay around $25,350 in annual out-of-pocket long-term care expenses, but, in reality, they'll more likely pay over $47,000.[10]

While local costs vary from state to state, here's the national median for various forms of long-term care (plus projections

---

9 Tara O'Neill Hayes, Sara Kurtovic. Americanactionforum.org. February 18, 2020. "The Ballooning Costs of Long-Term Care."
https://www.americanactionforum.org/research/the-ballooning-costs-of-long-term-care
10 Moll Law Group. 2021. "The Cost of Long-Term Care."
https://www.molllawgroup.com/the-cost-of-long-term-care.html

that account for a 3 percent annual inflation, so you can see what I am referencing):[11]

Long-Term Care Costs: Inflation				
	Home Health Care, Homemaker Services	Adult Day Care	Assisted Living	Nursing Home (semi-private room)
Annual 2021	$59,488	$20,280	$54,000	$94,900
Annual 2031	$79,947	$27,255	$72,571	$127,538
Annual 2041	$107,442	$36,628	$97,530	$171,400
Annual 2051	$144,393	$49,225	$131,072	$230,347

Fund Your Long-Term Care

One crucial mistake I see are those who haven't planned for long-term care because they assume the government will provide everything. But that's a big misconception. The government has two health insurance programs: Medicare and Medicaid. These can greatly assist you in your health care needs in retirement but usually don't provide enough coverage to cover all your health care costs in retirement. My firm isn't a government outpost, so we don't get to make decisions when it comes to forming policy and specifics about either one of these programs. I'm going to give an overview of both, but if you want

---

[11] Genworth Financial. January 2022. "Cost of Care Survey 2021." https://www.genworth.com/aging-and-you/finances/cost-of-care.html

to dive into the details of these programs, you can visit www.Medicare.gov and www.Medicaid.gov.

Medicare

Medicare covers those aged sixty-five and older and those who are disabled. Medicare's coverage of any nursing-home-related health issues is limited. It might cover your nursing home stay if it is not a "custodial" stay, and it isn't long-term. For example, if you break a bone or suffer a stroke, stay in a nursing home for rehabilitative care, and then return home, Medicare may cover you. But, if you have developed dementia or are looking to move to a nursing facility because you can no longer bathe, dress, toilet, feed yourself, or take care of your hygiene, etc., then Medicare is not going to pay for your nursing home costs.[12]

You can enroll in Medicare anytime during the three months before and three months after your sixty-fifth birthday. Miss your enrollment deadline, and you could risk paying increased premiums for the rest of your life.[13] On top of prompt enrollment, there are a few other things to think about when it comes to Medicare, not least among them being the need to understand the different "parts," what they do, and what they don't cover.

Part A

Medicare Part A is what you might think of as "classic" Medicare. Hospital care, some types of home health care, and major medical care fall under this. While most enrollees pay nothing for this service (as they likely paid into the system for at least ten years), you may end up paying, either based on work history or delayed signup. In 2022, the highest premium is

---

[12] Medicare.gov. "What Part A covers." https://www.medicare.gov/what-medicare-covers/part-a/what-part-a-covers.html

[13] Medicare.gov. "When can I sign up for Medicare?" https://www.medicare.gov/basics/get-started-with-medicare/sign-up/when-can-i-sign-up-for-medicare

$499 per month, and a hospital stay does have a deductible, $1,556.[14] And, if you have a hospital stay that surpasses sixty days, you could be looking at additional costs; keep in mind, Medicare doesn't pay for long-term care and services.

Part B

Medicare Part B is an essential piece of wrap-around coverage for Medicare Part A. It helps pay for doctor visits and outpatient services. This also comes with a price tag: Although the Part B deductible is only $233 in 2022, you will still pay 20 percent of all costs after that, with no limit on out-of-pocket expenses.[15]

Part C

Medicare Part C, more commonly known as Medicare Advantage plans, are an alternative to a combination of Parts A, B, and sometimes D. Administered through private insurance companies, these have a variety of costs and restrictions, and they are subject to the specific policies and rules of the issuing carrier.

Part D

Medicare Part D is also through a private insurer and is supplemental to Parts A and B, as its primary purpose is to cover prescription drugs. Like any private insurance plan, Part D has its quirks and rules that vary from insurer to insurer.

The Donut Hole

Even with a "Part D" in place, you may still have a coverage gap between what your Part D private drug insurance pays for your prescription and what basic Medicare pays. In 2022, the

---

[14] Medicare. "Medicare 2022 Costs at a Glance."
https://www.medicare.gov/your-medicare-costs/medicare-costs-at-a-glance
[15] Ibid.

coverage gap is $4,430, meaning, after you meet your private prescription insurance limit, you will spend no more than 25 percent of your drug costs out-of-pocket before Medicare will kick in to pay for more prescription drugs.[16]

Medicare Supplements

Medicare Supplement Insurance, MedSup, Medigap, or plans labeled Medicare Part F, G, H, I, J . . . Known by a variety of monikers, this is just a fancy way of saying "medical coverage for those over sixty-five that picks up the tab for whatever the federal Medicare program(s) doesn't." Again, costs, limitations, etc., vary by carrier.

Does that sound like a bunch of government alphabet soup to you? It certainly does to me. And, did you read the fine print? Unpredictable costs, varied restrictions, difficult-to-compare benefits, donut holes, and coverage gaps. That's par for the course with health care plans through the course of our adult lives. What gives? I thought Medicare was supposed to be easier, comprehensive, and at no cost!

The truth is there is no stage of life when health care is easy to understand.

I knew of a person who took too much out of their IRAs to do a Roth conversion. In their effort to save money on taxes, without proper preparation and scenario planning, their Medicare premium went up and stayed up for two years.

The best thing you can do for yourself is to scope out the health care field early, compare costs often, and prepare for out-of-pocket costs well in advance—decades, if possible.

---

[16] Medicare. "Costs in the coverage gap."
https://www.medicare.gov/drug-coverage-part-d/costs-for-medicare-drug-coverage/costs-in-the-coverage-gap

Medicaid

Medicaid is a program the states administer, so funding, protocol, and limitations vary. Compared to Medicare, Medicaid more widely covers nursing home care, but it targets a different demographic: those with low incomes.

If you have more assets than the Medicaid limit in your state and need nursing home care, you will need to use those assets to pay for your care. You will also have a list of additional state-approved ways to spend some of these assets over the Medicaid limit, such as pre-purchasing burial plots and funeral expenses or paying off debts. After that, your remaining assets fund your nursing home stay until they are gone, at which point Medicaid will jump in.

Some people aren't stymied by this, thinking they will just pass on their financial assets early, gifting them to relatives, friends, and causes so they can qualify for Medicaid when they need it. However, to prevent this exact scenario, Uncle Sam has implemented the look-back period. Currently, if you enroll in Medicaid, you are subject to having the government scrutinize the last five years of your finances for large gifts or expenses that may subject you to penalties, temporarily making you ineligible for Medicaid coverage.

So, if you're planning to preserve your money for future generations and retain control of your financial resources during your lifetime, you'll probably want to prepare for the costs of longevity beyond a "government plan."

Self-Funding

One way to fund a longer life is the old-fashioned way, through self-funding. There are a variety of financial tools you can use, and they all have their pros and cons. If your assets are in low-interest financial vehicles (savings, bonds, CDs), you risk letting inflation erode the value of your dollar. Or, if you are relying on the stock market, you have more growth potential, but you'll also want to consider the possible implications of market volatility. What if your assets take a hit? If you suffer a loss in your retirement portfolio in early or mid-retirement, you might have the option to "tighten your belt," so to speak, and cut back on discretionary spending to allow your portfolio the room to bounce back. But, if you are retired and depend on income from a stock account that just hit a downward stride, what are you going to do?

HSAs

These days, you might also be able to self-fund through a health savings account, or HSA, if you have access to one through a high-deductible health plan (you will not qualify to save in an HSA after enrolling in Medicare). In an HSA, any growth of your tax-deductible contributions will be tax-free, and any distributions paid out for qualified health costs are also tax-free. Long-term care expenses count as health costs, so, if this is an option available to you, it is one way to use the tax advantages to self-fund your longevity. Bear in mind, if you are younger than sixty-five, any money you use for nonqualified expenses will be subject to taxes and penalties, and, if you are older than sixty-five, any HSA money you use for non-medical expenses is subject to income tax.

LTCI

One slightly more nuanced way to pay for longevity, specifically for long-term care, is long-term care insurance, or LTCI. As car insurance protects your assets in case of a car accident and home insurance protects your assets in case something happens to your house, long-term care insurance aims to protect your assets in case you need long-term care in an at-home or nursing home situation.

As with other types of insurance, you will pay a monthly or annual premium in exchange for an insurance company paying for long-term care down the road. Typically, policies cover two to three years of care, which is adequate for an "average" situation: it's estimated 70 percent of Americans will need about three years of long-term care of some kind. However, it's important to consider you might not be "average" when you are preparing for long-term care costs; on average, 20 percent of today's sixty-five-year-olds could need care for longer than five years.[17]

Now, there are a few oft-cited components of LTCI that make it unattractive for some:

- Expense — LTCI can be expensive. It is generally less expensive the younger you are, but at the time of this writing, a fifty-five-year-old couple who purchased LTCI could expect to pay $2,080 each year for an average three-year coverage policy. And the annual cost only increases from there the older you are.[18]

- Limited options — Let's face it: LTCI may be expensive for consumers, but it can also be expensive for companies that offer it. With fewer companies willing to take on that expense, this narrows the market, meaning opportunities to price shop for policies with different options or custom benefits are limited.

- If you know you need it, you might not be able to get it — Insurance companies offering LTCI are taking on a risk that you may need LTCI. That risk is the foundation of the product — you may or may not need it. If you know you will need it because you have a dementia diagnosis or another illness for which you will need long-term care, you will likely not qualify for LTCI coverage.

- Use it or lose it — If you have LTCI and are in the minority of Americans who die having never needed long-term care, all the money you paid into your LTCI policy is gone.

- Possibly fluctuating rates—Your rate is not locked in on LTCI. Companies maintain the ability to raise or lower

---

[17] LongTermCare.gov. February 18, 2020. "How Much Care Will You Need?" https://acl.gov/ltc/basic-needs/how-much-care-will-you-need
[18] American Association for Long-Term Care Insurance. 2022. "Long-Term Care Insurance Facts-Data-Statistics-2022 Reports" https://www.aaltci.org/long-term-care-insurance/learning-center/ltcfacts-2022.php#2022costs

your premium amounts. This means some seniors face an ultimatum: Keep funding a policy at what might be a less affordable rate *or* lose coverage and let go of all the money they paid in so far.

After that, you might be thinking, "How can people possibly be interested in LTCI?" But let me repeat myself—as many as 70 percent of Americans will need long-term care. And, although only one in ten Americans age fifty-five-plus have purchased LTCI, keep in mind the high cost of nursing home care. Can you afford $7,000 a month to put into nursing home care and still have enough left over to protect your legacy? This is a very real concern considering one set of statistics reported a two-in-three chance that a senior citizen will become physically or cognitively impaired in their lifetime.[19] So, not to sound like a broken record, but it is vitally important to have a plan in place to deal with longevity and long-term care if you intend to leave a financial legacy.

A few relevant statistics to keep in mind:

- The longer you live, the more likely you are to continue living; the longer you live, the more health care you will likely need to pay for.

- The average cost of a private nursing home room in the United States in 2021 was $9,034 a month.[20] But keep in mind, that is just the nursing home—it doesn't include other medical costs, let alone pleasantries, like entertainment or hobby spending.

- In 2021, Fidelity calculated that a healthy couple retiring at age sixty-five could expect to pay around $300,000 over the course of retirement to cover health and medical expenses.

---

[19] payingforseniorcare.com. 2022. "Long-Term Senior Care Statistics" https://www.payingforseniorcare.com/statistics
[20] Genworth Financial. January 31, 2022. "Genworth 2020 Cost of Care Survey." https://www.genworth.com/aging-and-you/finances/cost-of-care.html

- The average man will need $143,000, and the average woman needs about 10 percent more, or $157,000, because of women's longer life expectancies.[21]

I know. Whoa, there, Mark, I was hoping to have a realistic idea of health costs, not be driven over by a cement mixer!

The good news is, while we don't know these exact costs in advance, we know there *will* be costs. And you won't have to pay your total Medicare lifetime premiums in one day as a lump sum. Now that you have a good idea of health care costs in retirement, you can *plan* for them! That's the real point, here: Planning in advance can keep you from feeling nickel-and-dimed to your wits' end. Instead, having a sizeable portion of your assets earmarked for health care can offer you greater freedom to choose health care networks, coverage options, and long-term care possibilities you like and that you think offer you the best in life.

Product Riders

LTCI and self-funding are not the only ways to plan for the expenses of longevity. Some companies are getting creative with their products, particularly insurance companies. One way they are retooling to meet people's needs is through optional product riders on annuities and life insurance. Elsewhere in this book, I talk about annuity basics, but here's a brief overview: Annuities are insurance contracts. You pay the insurance company a premium, either as a lump sum or as a series of payments over a set amount of time, in exchange for guaranteed income payments. One of the features of an annuity is it has access to riders, which allow you to tweak your contract for a fee, usually about 1 percent of the contract value annually. One annuity rider some companies offer is a long-term care

---

[21] Elizabeth O'Brien. Money. May 10, 2021. "Health Care Now Costs Couples $300,000 in Retirement, According to Fidelity's Latest Estimate." https://money.com/health-care-costs-retirement-fidelity-2021-study/

rider. If you have an annuity with a long-term care rider and are not in need of long-term care, your contract behaves as any annuity contract would—nothing changes. Generally speaking, if you reach a point when you can't perform multiple functions of daily life on your own, you notify the insurance company, and a representative will turn on those provisions of your contract.

Like LTCI, different companies and products offer different options. Some annuity long-term care riders offer coverage of two years in a nursing home situation. Others cap expenses at two times the original annuity's value. It greatly depends. Some people prefer this option because there isn't a "use-it-or-lose-it" piece; if you die without ever having needed long-term care, you still will have had the income benefit from the base contract. Still, as with any annuities or insurance contracts, there are the usual restrictions and limitations. Withdrawing money from the contract will affect future income payments, early distributions can result in a penalty, income taxes may apply, and, because the insurance company's solvency is what guarantees your payments, it's important to do your research about the insurance company you are considering purchasing a contract from.

Understandably, a discussion on long-term care is bound to feel at least a little tedious. Yet, this is a critical piece of planning for income in retirement, particularly if you want to leave a legacy.

For example, we have a client, who we'll call Fred, and he's currently an Uber driver. He was a successful business person who had plenty of money to retire, except for the fact that he failed to plan for long-term care needs. His wife went into the hospital for cancer, and due to medical bills and high deductibles, he was left with no money. He spent it all on health care needs, and he is now driving a taxi to make ends meet.

Spousal Planning

Here's one thing to keep in mind no matter how you plan to save: Many of us will be planning for more than ourselves. Look back at all the stats on health events and the likelihood of long life and long-term care. If they hold true for a single individual, then the likelihood of having a costly health or long-term care event is even higher for a married couple. You'll be planning for not just one life, but two. So, when it comes to long-term care insurance, annuities, self-funding, or whatever strategy you are looking at using, be sure you are funding longevity for the both of you.

CHAPTER 8

Taxes

Where to begin with taxes? Perhaps by acknowledging we all bear responsibility for the resources we share. Roads, bridges, schools . . . It is the patriotic duty of every American to pay their fair share of taxes. Many would agree with me.

Now, just talking taxes probably takes your mind to April—tax season. You are probably thinking about all the forms you collect and how you file. Perhaps you are thinking about your certified public accountant or another qualified tax professional and saying to yourself, "I've already got taxes taken care of, thanks!"

However, what I see when people come into my office is that their relationship with their tax professional is purely a January through April relationship. That means they may have a tax professional, but not a tax *planner.*

What I mean is tax planning extends beyond filing taxes. In April, we are required to settle our accounts with the IRS to make sure we have paid up on our bill or to even the score if we have overpaid. But real tax planning is about making each financial move in a way that allows you to keep the most money in your pocket and out of Uncle Sam's.

Now, as a caveat, I want to emphasize I am neither a CPA nor a tax planner, but I see the way taxes affect my clients, and I have plenty of experience helping clients implement tax-efficient strategies in their retirement plans in conjunction with their tax professionals.

I don't believe a financial advisor can truly say they cover all of the bases in retirement preparation if they do not do tax planning. In my opinion, knowing how to reduce taxes and use your assets in a tax-efficient manner is one of the most important aspects of financial planning.

It is especially important to me to help my clients develop tax-efficient strategies in their retirement plans because each dollar they can keep in their pockets is a dollar we can put to work.

While writing this in 2022, the national deficit continues to skyrocket, as though we will never have to pay it back. It's highly likely taxes will rise in 2025 when the Trump tax plan (Tax Cuts and Jobs Act, or TCJA) sunsets, especially when you consider the need to pay back the exoribitant government spending we've seen in recent years.

The Fed

Now, in the United States, taxes can be a rather uncertain proposition. Depending on who is in the White House and which party controls Congress, we might be tempted to assume tax rates could either decline or increase in the next four to eight years accordingly. However, there is one (large!) factor we, as a nation, must confront: the national debt.

Currently, according to USDebtClock.org, we are over $30,000,000,000,000 in debt and climbing. That's $30 *trillion* with a "T." With just $1 trillion, you could park it in the bank at a zero percent interest rate and spend more than $54 million every day for fifty years without hitting a zero balance.

Even if Congress got a handle and stopped that debt from its daily compound, divided by each taxpayer, we each would owe about $214,000. So, will that be check, cash, or Venmo?

My point here isn't to give you anxiety. I'm just cautioning you that even with the rosiest of outlooks on our personal income tax rates, none of us should count on low tax rates for the long term. Instead, you and your network of professionals (tax, legal, and financial) should constantly be looking for ways to take advantage of tax-saving opportunities as they come. After all, the best "luck" is when proper planning meets opportunity.

So, how can we get started?

Know Your Limits

One of the foundational pieces of tax planning is knowing what tax bracket you are in, based on your income after subtracting pre-tax or untaxed assets. Your income taxes are based on your taxable income.

One reason to know your taxable income and your income tax rate is so you can see how far away you are from the next lower or higher tax bracket. This is particularly important when it comes to decisions such as gifting and Roth IRA rollovers.

For instance, based on the 2022 tax table, Mallory and Ralph's taxable income is just over $345,000, putting them in the 32 percent tax bracket and about $4,900 above the upper end of the 24 percent tax bracket. They have already maxed out their retirement funds' tax-exempt contributions for the year. Their daughter, Gloria, is a sophomore in college. This couple could shave a considerable amount off their tax bill if they use the $4,900 to help Gloria out with groceries and school—something they were likely to do, anyway, but now can deliberately be put to work for them in their overall financial strategy.

Now, I use Mallory and Ralph only as an example—your circumstances are probably different—but I think this nicely illustrates the way planning ahead for taxes can potentially save you money.

Assuming a Lower Tax Rate

Many people anticipate being in a lower tax bracket in retirement. It makes sense: You won't be contributing to retirement funds; you'll be drawing from them. And you won't have all those work expenses—work clothes, transportation, lunch meetings, etc.

Yet, do you really plan on changing your lifestyle after retirement? Do you plan to cut down on the number of times you eat out, scale back vacations, and skimp on travel?

What I see in my office is many couples spend more in the first few years, or maybe the first decade, of retirement. Sure, that may taper off later on, but usually only just in time for their budget to be hit with greater health and long-term care expenses. Do you see where this is going? Many people plan as though their taxable income will be lower in retirement and are surprised when the tax bills come in and look more or less the same as they used to. It's better to plan for the worst and hope for the best, wouldn't you agree?

401(k)/IRA

One sometimes-unexpected piece of tax planning in retirement concerns your 401(k) or IRA. Most of us have one of these accounts or an equivalent. Throughout our working lives, we pay in, dutifully socking away a portion of our earnings in these tax-deferred accounts. There's the rub: tax-deferred. Not tax-free. Very rarely is anything free of taxation when you get down to it. Using 401(k)s and IRAs in retirement is no different. The taxes the government deferred when you were in your working years are now coming due, and you will pay taxes on that income at whatever your current tax rate is.

Just to ensure Uncle Sam gets his due, the government also has a required minimum distribution, or RMD, rule. Beginning at age seventy-two, you are required to withdraw a certain minimum amount every year from your 401(k) or IRA, or else you will face a 50 percent tax penalty on any RMD monies you should have withdrawn but didn't—and that's on top of income tax.

Of course, there is also the Roth account. You can think of the difference between a Roth and a traditional retirement account as the difference between taxing the seed and taxing the harvest. Because Roths are funded with post-tax dollars, there aren't tax penalties for early withdrawals of the principal nor are there taxes on the growth after you reach age fifty-nine-and-one-half. Perhaps best of all, there are no RMDs. Of course, you must own a Roth account for a minimum of five years before you are able to take advantage of all its features.

This is one more area where it pays to be aware of your tax bracket. Some people may find it advantageous to "convert" their traditional retirement account funds to Roth account funds in a year during which they are in a lower tax bracket. Others may opt to put any excess RMDs from their traditional retirement accounts into other products, like stocks or insurance.

Does that make your head spin? Understandable. That's why it's so important to work with a financial professional and tax planner who can help you execute these sorts of tax-efficient strategies and help you understand what you are doing and why.

Sometimes it doesn't take much to make the leap to a higher tax bracket. It's important to make any financial decisions with a strategy in mind so you don't inadvertently cost yourself thousands of dollars in taxes or other avoidable costs.

CHAPTER 9

Retirement Income

R etirement. For many of us, it's what we've saved for and dreamed of, pinning our hopes to a magical someday. Is that someday full of traveling? Is it filled with grandkids? Gardening? Maybe your fondest dream is simply never having to work again, never having to clock in or be accountable to someone else.

Your ability to do these things all hinges on *income*. Without the money to support these dreams, even a basic level of work-free lifestyle is unsustainable. That's why planning for your income in retirement is so foundational. But where do we begin?

It's easy to feel overwhelmed by this question. Some may feel the urge to amass a large lump sum and then try to put it all in one product—insurance, investments, liquid assets—to provide all the growth, liquidity, and income they need. Instead, I think most people need a more balanced approach. After all, retirement planning isn't magic. Like I mention elsewhere, there is no single product that can be all things to all people (or even all things to one person). No approach works unilaterally for everyone. That's why it's important to talk to a financial professional who can help you lay down the basics and take you step-by-step through the process. Not only will you have the assurance you have addressed the areas you need to, but you will also have an ally who can help you break down the process and help keep you from feeling overwhelmed.

Sources of Income

Thinking of all the pieces of your retirement expenses might be intimidating. But, like cleaning out a junk drawer or revisiting that garage remodel, once you have laid everything out, you can begin to sort things into categories.

Once you have a good overall picture of where your expenses will lie, you can start stacking up the resources to cover them.

Social Security

Social Security is a guaranteed, inflation-protected federal program playing a significant part in most of our retirement plans. From delaying until you've reached full retirement age or beyond to examining spousal benefits, as I discuss elsewhere in this book, there is plenty you can do to try to make the most of this monthly benefit. As with all your retirement income sources, it's important to consider how to make this resource stretch to provide the most bang and buck for your situation.

Pension

Another generally reliable source of retirement income for you might be a pension, if you are one of the lucky people who still has one.

If you don't have a pension, go ahead and skim on to the next section. If you do have a pension, keep on reading.

Because your pension can be such a central piece of your retirement income plan, you will want to put some thought into answering basic questions about it.

How well is your pension funded? Since the heyday of the pension plan, companies and governments have neglected to fund their pension obligations, causing a persistent problem with this otherwise reliable asset. However, research conducted by the Pew Charitable Trusts showed a collective increase in assets exceeding half a trillion dollars in state retirement plans fueled by strong market investment returns in fiscal 2021.

Pew's estimates that state retirement systems rose to 80 percent funding for the first time in 2008.[22]

Consider the factors at play, though. Pensions had been underfunded and gained a boost from strong market performance in 2021. What happens to the solvency of those pension funds if the market declines?

It can be worthwhile to keep tabs on your pension's health and know what your options are for withdrawing your pension. If you have already retired and made those decisions, this may be a foregone conclusion. If not, it pays to know what you can expect and what decisions you can make, such as taking spousal options to cover your husband or wife if he or she outlives you.

Also, some companies are incentivizing lump-sum payouts of pensions to reduce the companies' payment liabilities. If that's the case with your employer, talk to your financial professional to see if it might be prudent to do something like that or if it might be better to stick with lifetime payments or other options.

Your 401(k) and IRA

One "modern way" to save for retirement is in a 401(k) or IRA (or their nonprofit or governmental equivalents). These tax-advantaged accounts are, in my opinion, a poor substitute for pensions, but one of the biggest disservices we do to ourselves is to not take full advantage of them in the first place. According to one article, only 32 percent of Americans invest in a 401(k), though 59 percent of employed Americans have access to a 401(k) benefit option.[23]

---

22 pewtrusts.org. September 14, 2021. "The State Pension Funding Gap: Plans Have Stabilized in Wake of Pandemic"
https://www.pewtrusts.org/en/research-and-analysis/issue-briefs/2021/09/the-state-pension-funding-gap-plans-have-stabilized-in-wake-of-pandemic
23 Amin Dabit. personalcapital.com. April 1, 2021. "The Average 401k Balance by Age." https://www.personalcapital.com/blog/retirement-planning/average-401k-balance-age

Also, if you have changed jobs over the years, do the work of tracking down any benefits from your past employers. You might have an IRA here or a 401(k) there; keep track of those so you can pull them together and look at those assets when you're ready to look at establishing sources of retirement income.

Do You Have...

- Life insurance?
- Annuities?
- Long-term care insurance?
- Any passive income sources?
- Stock and bond portfolios?
- Liquid assets? (What's in your bank account?)
- Alternative investments?
- Rental properties?

If you are going through the work of sitting with a financial professional, it's important to look at your full retirement income picture and pull together *all* your assets, no matter how big or small. From the free insurance policy offered at your bank to the sizable investment in your brother-in-law's modestly successful furniture store, you want to have a good idea of where your money is.

I know a person who hated her job. It turns out that once she reviewed her assets carefully, she was actually able to extract sufficient income from the investments and even retire that next week.

Retirement Income Needs

How much income will you need in retirement? How do you determine that? A lot of people work toward a random number, thinking, "If I can just have a million dollars, I'll be comfortable in retirement!" Don't get me wrong; it is possible to save up a lot of money and then retire in the hopes you can keep your monthly expenses lower than some set estimation. But I think this carries a general risk of running out of money. Instead, I work with my clients to find out what their current and projected income needs are and then work from there to see how we might cover any gaps between what they have and what they want.

Goals and Dreams

I like to start with your pie in the sky. Do you find yourself planning for your vacations more thoroughly than you do your retirement? It's not uncommon for Americans to spend more time planning our vacations than we spend planning our retirements. Maybe it's because planning a vacation is less stressful: Having a week at the beach go awry is, well, a walk on the beach compared to running out of money in retirement. Whatever the case, perhaps it would be better if you thought of your retirement as a vacation in and of itself—no clocking in, no boss, no overtime. If you felt unlimited by financial strain, what would you do?

Would an endless vacation for you mean Paris and Rome? Would it mean mentoring at children's clubs or serving at the local soup kitchen? Or maybe it would mean deepening your ties to those immediately around you—neighbors, friends, and family. Maybe it would mean more time to take part in the hobbies and activities you love. Have you been considering a second (or even third) act as a small-business owner, turning a hobby or passion into a revenue source?

This is your time to daydream and answer the question: If you could do anything, what would you do?

After that, it's a matter of putting a dollar amount on it. What are the costs of round-the-world travel? One couple I know said their highest priority in retirement was being able to take each of their grandchildren on a cross-country vacation every year. That's a pretty specific goal—one that is reasonably easy to nail down a budget for.

We have a client who wanted to retire early. We were able to take a look at his income situation and tell him that, thanks to the savings he'd accumulated, he could retire that very day. He and his wife are now currently retired at age fifty-five and fifty-seven, living in the Lake of the Ozarks.

Current Budget

Compiling a current expense report is one of the trickiest pieces of retirement preparation. Many people assume the expenses of their lives in retirement will be different—lower. After all, there will be no drive to work, no need for a formal wardrobe, and, perhaps most impactful of all, no more saving for retirement!

Yet, we often underestimate our daily spending habits. That's why I typically ask my clients to bring in their bank statements for the past year—they are reflective of your *actual* spending, not just what you think you're spending.

We have our clients run through a budget prior to retiring so they can determine their income needs in retirement.

I can't count the number of times I have sat with a couple, asked them about their spending, and heard them throw out a number that seemed incredibly low. When I ask them where the number came from, they usually say they estimated based on their total bills. Yet, our spending is so much more than our mortgage, utilities, cable, phone, car, grocery, or credit card bills.

"What about clothes?" I ask, "Or dining out? What about gifts and coffees and last-minute birthday cards?" That's when the lights come on.

This is why I suggest collecting a year's worth of information. There is usually no such thing as a one-time purchase. Did you buy new furniture? Even if that is a rarity, do you think that will be the last time you *ever* buy furniture?

I gave a presentation on budgeting, and I had a client who was amazed that after two months of budgeting, he was able to discover an additional $600 a month in his budget.

Another hefty expense is spending on the kids. Many of the couples I work with are quick to help their adult children, whether it's something like letting them live in the basement, paying for college, babysitting, paying an occasional bill, or contributing to a grandchild's college fund. Research concluded that 22 percent of adults receive some kind of financial support from parents. That segment jumps to almost 30 percent when factoring the generation we call millennials.[24]

My clients sometimes protest that what they do for their grown children can stop in retirement. They don't *need* to help. But I get it. Parents like to feel needed. And, while you never want to neglect saving for retirement in favor of taking on financial risks (like your child's student debt), the parents who help their adult children do so in part because it helps them feel fulfilled.

When it comes down to expenses, including (and especially) spending on your family, don't make your initial calculations based on what you *could* whittle your budget down to if you *had* to. Instead, start from where you are. Who wants to live off a bare-bones bank account in retirement?

Other Expenses

Once you have nailed down your current budget and your dreams or goals for retirement, there are a few other outstanding pieces to think about—some expenses many people don't take the time to consider before making and executing a plan. But I'm assuming you want to get it right, so let's take a look.

---

[24] Kamaron McNair. magnifymoney.com. October 26, 2021. "Nearly 30% of Millenials Still Receive Financial Support From Their Parents" https://www.magnifymoney.com/blog/news/parental-financial-support-survey/

Housing

Do you know where you want to live in retirement? This makes up a substantial piece of your income puzzle—since the typical American household owns a home, and it's generally their largest asset.

Some people prefer to live right where they are for as long as they can. Others have been waiting for retirement to pull the trigger on an ambitious move, like purchasing a new house, or even downsizing. Whatever your plans and whatever your reasons, there are quite a few things to consider.

Mortgage

Do you still have a mortgage? What may have been a nice tax boon in your working years could turn into a financial burden in your retirement. After all, when you are on a limited income, a mortgage is just one more bill sapping your financial strength. It is something to put some thought into, whether you plan to age in place or are considering moving to your dream home, buying a house out of state, or living in a retirement community.

Upkeep and Taxes

A house without a mortgage still requires annual taxes. While it's tempting to think of this as a once-a-year expense, when you have limited earning potential, your annual tax bill might be something into which you should put a little more forethought.

The costs of homeownership aren't just monetary. When you find yourself dealing with more house than you need, it can drain your time and energy. From keeping clutter at bay to keeping the lawn mower running, upkeep can be extensive and expensive. For some, that's a challenge they heartily accept and can comfortably take on. For others, the idea of yard work or cleaning an area larger than they need feels foolish.

For instance, Peggy discovered after her knee replacement that most of her house was inaccessible to her when she was laid up.

"It felt ridiculous to pay someone else to dust and vacuum a house I was only living in 40 percent of!"

Practicality and Adaptability

Erik and Magda are looking to retire within the next two decades. They just sold their old three-bedroom ranch-style house. Their twins are in high school, and the couple has wanted to "upgrade" for years. Now they live in a gorgeous 1940s three-story house with all the kitchen space they ever wanted, five sprawling bedrooms, and a library and media room for themselves and their children. Within months of moving in, the couple realized a house perfect for their active teens would no longer be perfect for them in five to fifteen years.

"We are paying the mortgage for this house, but we've started saving for the next one," said Magda, "because who wants to climb two flights of stairs to their bedroom when they're seventy-eight?"

Others I know have encountered a similar situation in their personal lives. After a health crisis, one couple found the luxurious tub for two they toiled to install had become a specter of a bad slip and a potential safety risk. It's important to think through what your physical reality could be. I always emphasize to my clients that they should plan for whatever their long-term future might hold, but it's amazing how many people don't give it much thought.

Contracts and Regulations

If you are looking into a cross-country move, be aware of new tax tables or local ordinances in the area where you are looking to move. After all, you don't want to experience sticker-shock when you are looking at downsizing or reducing your bills in retirement.

Along the same lines, if you are moving into a retirement community, be sure to look at the fine print. What happens if you must move into a different situation for long-term care?

Will you be penalized? Will you be responsible for replacing your slot in the community? What are all the fees, and what do they cover?

Inflation

As I write this in 2022, America has experienced a wave of inflation following a lengthy period of low inflation. Inflation zoomed to 9.1 percent in June 2022, its highest mark since November 1981.[25]

Core inflation is yet another measurement that excludes goods with prices that tend to be more volatile, such as food and energy costs. Core inflation for a 12-month period ending in June 2022 was 5.9 percent. It so happened energy prices rose a whopping 41.6 percent over that timeframe.[26]

However, inflation isn't a one-time bump; it has a cumulative effect. Again, that can impact the price of groceries greater than other goods. Even with relatively low inflation over the past few decades, an item you bought in 1997 for two dollars will cost $3.60 today.[27] Want to go to a show? A $20 ticket in 1997 would cost $40.34 in 2022.[28]

What if, in retirement, we hit a stretch like the late seventies and early eighties, when annual inflation rates of 10 percent became the norm? It may be wise to consider some extra padding in your retirement income plan to account for any potential increase in inflation in the future.

---

[25] tradingeconomics.com. 2022 Data/2023 Forecast/1914-2021 Historical. "United States Inflation Rate" https://tradingeconomics.com/united-states/inflation-cpi

[26] U.S. Inflation Calculator. "United States Core Inflation Rates (1957-2022)" https://www.usinflationcalculator.com/inflation/united-states-core-inflation-rates

[27] Ibid.

[28] In2013dollars.com "Admission to movies, theaters, and concerts priced at $20 in 1997>$40.34 in 2022" https://www.in2013dollars.com/Admission-to-movies,-theaters,-and-concerts/price-inflation

Aging

Also, in the expense category, think about longevity. We all hope to age gracefully. However, it's important to face the prospect of aging with a sense of realism.

The elephant in the room for many families is long-term care. No one wants to admit they will likely need it, but estimates indicate almost 70 percent of us will.[29] Aging is a significant piece of retirement income planning because you'll want to figure out how to set aside money for your care, either at home or away from it. The more comfortable you get with discussing your wishes and plans with your loved ones, the easier planning for the financial side of it can be.

I denote health care and potential long-term care costs in more detail elsewhere in this book, but suffice it to say nursing home care tends to be expensive and typically isn't something you get to choose when you will need.

It isn't just the costs of long-term care that pose a concern in living longer. It's also about covering the possible costs of everything else associated with living longer. For instance, if Henry retires from his job as a biochemical engineer at age sixty-five, perhaps he planned to have a very decent income for twenty years, until age eighty-five. But what if he lives until he's ninety-five? That's a whole third—ten years—more of personal income he will need.

Putting It All Together

Whew! So, you have pulled together what you have, and you have a pretty good idea of where you want to be. Now your financial professional and you can go about the work of arranging what assets you *have* to cover what you *need*—and how you might try to cover any gaps.

---

[29] Moll Law Group. 2022. "The Cost of Long-Term Care."
https://www.molllawgroup.com/the-cost-of-long-term-care.html

Like the proverbial man in the Bible who built his house on a rock, I like to help my clients figure out how to cover their day-to-day living expenses—their needs—with insurance and other income sources like pensions and Social Security.

The first step is to determine how much income they need. I believe any good retirement plan starts with this step. Second, we determine how much they have, and third, how much risk they are willing to take. Finally, we show them how to derive enough income from this to meet their income needs, then show them how to help protect it with LTC and estate planning.

Again, you should keep in mind there isn't one single financial vehicle, asset, or source to fill all your needs, and that's okay. One of the challenges of planning for your income in retirement concerns figuring out what products and strategies to use. You can release some of that stress when you accept the fact you will probably need a diverse portfolio—potentially with bonds, stocks, insurance, and other income sources—not just one massive money pile.

One way to help shore up your income gaps is by working with your financial professional and a qualified tax advisor to mitigate your tax exposure. If you have a 401(k) or IRA, a tax advisor in your corner can help you figure out how and when to take distributions from your account in a way that could help prevent you from entering into a higher tax bracket. Or you might learn how to use tax-advantaged bonds more effectively. Effective tax planning isn't necessarily about "adding" to your income. Especially regarding retirement, it's less about what you make than it is about what you keep. Paying a lower tax bill keeps more money in your pocket, which is where you want it when it comes to retirement income.

Now you can look at ways to cover your remaining retirement goals. Are there products like long-term care insurance specific to a certain kind of expense you anticipate? Is there a particular asset you want to use for your "play" money—money for trips and gifts for the grandkids? Is there any way you can portion off money for those charitable legacy plans?

Once you have analyzed your income wants, needs, and the assets to realistically cover them, you may have a gap. The masterstroke of a competent financial professional will be to help you figure out how you will cover that gap. Will you need to cut out a round of golf a week? Maybe skip the new car? Or will you need to take more substantial action?

One way to cover an income gap is to consider working longer or even part-time before retirement and even after that magical calendar date. This may not be the best "plan" for you; disabilities, work demands, and physical or emotional limitations can hinder the best-laid plans to continue working. However, if it is physically possible for you, this is one considerable way to help your assets last, for more than one reason.

In fact, 46 percent of the Americans responding to a survey report they plan to work part-time after retiring, while 18 percent indicated they planned to work past the age of seventy.[30]

When you're retired, you no longer have an employer paying you a steady check. It is up to you to make sure you have saved and planned for the income you need.

---

[30] Palash Ghosh. Forbes.com. May 6, 2021. "A Third Of Seniors Seek To Work Well Past Retirement Age, Or Won't Retire At All, Poll Finds" https://www.forbes.com/sites/palashghosh/2021/05/06/a-third-of-seniors-seek-to-work-well-past-retirement-age-or-wont-retire-at-all-poll-finds/?sh=1d2ece836b95

CHAPTER 10

Social Security

Social Security is often the foundation of retirement income. Backed by the strength of the U.S. Treasury, it provides perhaps the most dependable income you will have in retirement.

From the time you collect your first paycheck from the job that made you a bonafide taxpayer (for me, it was mowing lawns in Florida when I was sixteen), you are paying into the grand old Social Security system. What grew and developed out of the pressures of the Great Depression has become one of the most popular government programs in the country, and, if you pay in for the equivalent of ten years or more, you, too, can benefit from the Social Security program.

Now, before we get into the nitty-gritty of Social Security, I'd like to address a current concern: Will Social Security still be there for you when you reach retirement age?

The Future of Social Security

This question is ever-present as headlines trumpet an underfunded Social Security program, alongside the sea of baby boomers retiring in droves and the comparatively smaller pool of younger people who are funding the system.

The Social Security Administration itself acknowledges this concern as each Social Security statement now bears an asterisk that continues near the end of the summary:

*"*Your estimated benefits are based on current law. Congress has made changes to the law in the past and can do so at any time. The law governing benefit amounts may change because, by 2034, the payroll taxes collected will be enough to pay only about 79 percent of scheduled benefits."*

Just a reminder, as if you needed one, that nothing in life is guaranteed. Additionally, depending on who you're listening to, Social Security funds may run low before 2034 thanks to the financial instability and government spending that accompanied the COVID-19 pandemic.

Before you get too discouraged, though, here are a few thoughts to keep you going:

- Even if the program is only paying 79 cents on the dollar for scheduled benefits, 79 percent is notably not zero.
- The Social Security Administration has made changes in the distant and near past to protect the fund's solvency, including increasing retirement ages and striking certain filing strategies.
- There are many changes Congress could make, and lawmakers routinely discuss how to fix the system, such as further increasing full retirement age and eligibility.
- One thing no one is seriously discussing? Reneging on current obligations to retirees or the soon-to-retire.

Take heart. The real answer to the question, "Will Social Security be there for me?" is still yes.

This question is important to consider when you look at how much we, as a nation, rely on this program. Did you know Social Security benefits replace about 40 percent of a person's original income when they retire?[31]

---

[31] ssa.gov. "Alternate Measure of Replacement Rates for Social Security Benefits and Retirement Income"
https://www.ssa.gov/policy/docs/ssb/v68n2/v68n2p1.html

If you ask me, that's a pretty significant piece of your retirement income puzzle.

Another caveat? You may not realize this, but no one can legally "advise" you about your Social Security benefits.

"But, Mark," you may be thinking, "isn't that part of what you do? And what about that nice gentleman at the Social Security Administration office I spoke with on the phone?"

Don't get me wrong. Social Security Administration employees know their stuff. They are trained to understand policies and programs, and they are usually pretty quick to tell you what you can and cannot do. But the government specifically stipulates, because Social Security is a benefit you alone have paid into and earned, your Social Security decisions, too, are yours alone.

When it comes to financial professionals, we can't push you in any direction, but—there's a big but here—working with a well-informed financial professional is still incredibly handy for your Social Security decisions. Why? Because someone who's worth his or her salt will know what withdrawal strategies might pertain to your specific situation and will ask questions that can help you determine what you are looking for when it comes to your Social Security.

For instance, some people want the highest possible monthly benefit. Others want to start their benefits early, not always because of financial need. I heard about one man who called in to start his Social Security payments the day he qualified, just because he liked to think of it as the government paying back a debt it owed him, and he enjoyed the feeling of receiving a check from Uncle Sam.

Whatever your reasons, questions, or feelings regarding Social Security, the decision is yours alone; but working with a financial professional can help you put your options in perspective by showing you—both with industry knowledge and with proprietary software or planning processes—where your benefits fit into your overall strategy for retirement income.

One reason the federal government doesn't allow for "advice" related to Social Security, I suspect, is so no one can profit from giving you advice related to your Social Security benefit—or from providing any clarifications. Again, this is a sign of a good financial professional. Those who are passionate about their work will be knowledgeable about what benefit strategies might be to your advantage and will happily share those possible options with you.

Full Retirement Age

When it comes to Social Security, it seems like many people only think so far as "yes." They don't take the time to understand the various options available. Instead, because it is common knowledge you can begin your benefits at age sixty-two, that's what many of us do. While more people are opting to delay taking benefits, age sixty-two is still firmly the most popular age to start.[32]

What many people fail to understand is, by starting benefits early, they may be leaving a lot of money on the table. You see, the Social Security Administration bases your monthly benefit on two factors: your earnings history and your full retirement age (FRA).

From your earnings history, they pull the thirty-five years you made the most money and use a mathematical indexing formula to figure out a monthly average from those years. If you paid into the system for less than thirty-five years, then every year you didn't pay in will be counted as a zero.

Once they have calculated what your monthly earning would be at FRA, the government then calculates what to put on your check based on how close you are to FRA. FRA was originally set at sixty-five, but, as the population aged and lifespans lengthened, the government shifted FRA later and later, based

---

[32] Chris Kissell. moneytalknews.com. January 20, 2021. "This Is When the Most People Start Taking Social Security." https://www.moneytalksnews.com/the-most-popular-age-for-claiming-social-security

on an individual's year of birth. Check out the following chart to see when you will reach FRA.[33]

Age to Receive Full Social Security Benefits*	
(Called "full retirement age" [FRA] or "normal retirement age.")	
Year of Birth*	FRA
1937 or earlier	65
1938	65 and 2 months
1939	65 and 4 months
1940	65 and 6 months
1941	65 and 8 months
1942	65 and 10 months
1943-1954	66
1955	66 and 2 months
1956	66 and 4 months
1957	66 and 6 months
1958	66 and 8 months
1959	66 and 10 months
1960 and later	67

If you were born on Jan. 1 of any year, you should refer to the previous year. (If you were born on the 1st of the month, we figure your benefit [and your full retirement age] as if your birthday was in the previous month.)

---

[33] Social Security Administration. "Full Retirement Age." https://www.ssa.gov/planners/retire/retirechart.html

When you reach FRA, you are eligible to receive 100 percent of whatever the Social Security Administration says is your full monthly benefit.

Starting at age sixty-two, for every year before FRA you claim benefits, your monthly check is reduced by 5 percent or more. Conversely, for every year you delay taking benefits past FRA, your monthly benefit increases by 8 percent (until age seventy—after that, there is no monetary advantage to delaying Social Security benefits). While your circumstances and needs may vary, a lot of financial professionals still urge people to at least consider delaying until they reach age seventy.

Why wait?[34]

Taking benefits early could affect your monthly check by ______.								
62	63	64	65	FRA 66	67	68	69	70
-25%	-20%	-13.3%	-6.7%	0	+8%	+16%	+24%	+32%

My Social Security

If you are over age thirty, you have probably received a notice from the Social Security Administration telling you to activate something called "My Social Security." This is a handy way to learn more about your particular benefit options, to keep track of what your earnings record looks like, and to calculate the benefits you have accrued over the years.

Essentially, My Social Security is an online account you can activate to see what your personal Social Security picture looks like, which you can do at www.ssa.gov/myaccount. This can be extremely helpful when it comes to planning for income in retirement and figuring up the difference between your anticipated income versus anticipated expenses.

---

[34] Social Security Administration. April 2021. "Can You Take Your Benefits Before Full Retirement Age?"
https://www.ssa.gov/planners/retire/applying2.html

COLA

Social Security is a largely guaranteed piece of the retirement puzzle: If you get a statement that reads you should expect $1,000 a month, you can be sure you will receive $1,000 a month. But there is one variable detail, and that is something called the cost-of-living adjustment, or COLA.

The COLA is an increase in your monthly check meant to address inflation in everyday life. After all, your expenses will likely continue to experience inflation in retirement, but you will no longer have the opportunity for raises, bonuses, or promotions you had when you were working. Instead, Social Security receives an annual cost-of-living increase tied to the Department of Labor's Consumer Price Index for Urban Wage Earners and Clerical Workers, or CPI-W. If the CPI-W measurement shows inflation rose a certain amount for regular goods and services, then Social Security recipients will see that reflected in their COLA.

The COLA averages 4 percent, but in a no- or low-inflation environment, such as in 2010, 2011, and 2016, Social Security recipients will not receive an adjustment. Some view the COLA as a perk, bump, or bonus, but, in reality, it works more like this: Your mom sends you to the store with $2.50 for a gallon of milk. Milk costs exactly $2.50. The next week, you go back with that same amount, but it is now $2.52 for a gallon, so you go back to Mom, and she gives you 2 cents. You aren't bringing home more milk—it just costs more money.

So the COLA is less about "making more money" and more about keeping seniors' purchasing power from eroding when inflation is a big factor, such as in 1975, when it was 8 percent![35] Still, don't let that detract from your enthusiasm about COLAs; after all, what if Mom's solution was: "Here's the same $2.50; try to find pennies from somewhere else to get that milk!"?

---

[35] Social Security Administration. "Cost-Of-Living Adjustment (COLA) Information for 2022." https://www.ssa.gov/cola

Spousal Benefits

We've talked about FRA, but another big Social Security decision involves spousal benefits.

If you or your spouse has a long stretch of zeros in your earnings history—perhaps if one of you stayed home for years, caring for children or sick relatives—you may want to consider filing for spousal benefits instead of filing on your own earnings history. A spousal benefit can be up to 50 percent of the primary wage earner's benefit at full retirement age.

To begin drawing a spousal benefit, you must be at least sixty-two years old, and the primary wage earner must have already filed for his or her benefit. While there are penalties for taking spousal benefits early (you could lose up to 67.5 percent of your check for filing at age sixty-two), you cannot earn credits for delaying past full retirement age.[36]

Like I wrote, the spousal benefit can be a big deal for those who don't have a very long pay history, but it's important to weigh your own earned benefits against the option of withdrawing based on a fraction of your spouse's benefits.

To look at how this could play out, let's use a hypothetical couple: Mary Jane, who is sixty, and Peter, who is sixty-two.

Let's say Peter's benefit at FRA, in his case sixty-six, would be $1,600. If Peter begins his benefits right now, four years before FRA, his monthly check will be $1,200. If Mary Jane begins taking spousal benefits in two years at the earliest date possible, her monthly benefits will be reduced by 67.5 percent, to $520 per month (remember, at FRA, the most she can qualify for is half of Peter's FRA benefit).

What if Peter and Mary Jane both wait until FRA? At sixty-six, Peter begins taking his full benefit of $1,600 a month. Two years later, when she reaches age sixty-six, Mary Jane will qualify for $800 a month. By waiting until FRA, the couple's monthly benefit goes from $1,720 to $2,400.

---

[36] Social Security Administration. "Retirement Planner: Benefits For You As A Spouse." https://www.ssa.gov/planners/retire/applying6.html

What if Peter delays until age seventy to get his maximum possible benefit? For each year past FRA he delays, his monthly benefits increase by 8 percent. This means, at seventy, he could file for a monthly benefit of $2,176. However, delayed retirement credits do not affect spousal benefits, so as soon as Peter files at seventy, Mary Jane would also file (at age sixty-eight) for her maximum benefit of $800, so their highest possible combined monthly check is $2,976.[37]

When it comes to your Social Security benefits, you obviously will want to consider whether a monthly check based on a fraction of your spouse's earnings will be comparable to or larger than your own earnings history.

Divorced Spouses

There are a few considerations for those of us who have gone through a divorce. If you 1) were married for ten years or more *and* 2) have since been divorced for at least two years *and* 3) are unmarried *and* 4) your ex-spouse qualifies to begin Social Security, you qualify for a spousal benefit based on your ex-husband or ex-wife's earnings history at FRA. A divorced spousal benefit is different from the married spousal benefit in one way: You don't have to wait for your ex-spouse to file before you can file yourself.[38]

For instance, Charles and Moira were married for fifteen years before their divorce, when he was thirty-six and she was forty. Moira has been remarried for twenty years, and, although Charles briefly remarried, his second marriage ended after a few years. Charles' benefits are largely calculated based on his many years of volunteering in schools, meaning his personal monthly benefit is close to zero.

---

[37] Office of the Chief Actuary. Social Security Administration. "Social Security Benefits: Benefits for Spouses." https://www.ssa.gov/OACT/quickcalc/spouse.html#calculator
[38] Social Security Administration. "Retirement Planner: If You Are Divorced." https://www.ssa.gov/planners/retire/divspouse.html

Although Moira has deferred her retirement, opting to delay benefits until she is seventy, Charles can begin taking benefits calculated from Moira's work history at FRA as early as sixty-two. However, he will also have the option of waiting until FRA to collect the maximum, or 50 percent of Moira's earned monthly benefit at her FRA.

Widowed Spouses

If your marriage ended with the death of your spouse, you might claim a benefit for your spouse's earned income as his or her widow/widower, called a survivor's benefit. Unlike a spousal benefit or divorced benefits, if your husband or wife dies, you can claim his or her full benefit. Also, unlike spousal benefits, if you need to, you can begin taking income when you turn sixty. However, as with other benefit options, your monthly check will be permanently reduced for withdrawing benefits before FRA.

If your spouse began taking benefits before he or she died, you can't delay withdrawing your survivor's benefits to get delayed credits. The Social Security Administration maintains you can only get as much from a survivor's benefit as your deceased spouse might have received, had he or she lived.[39]

Taxes, Taxes, Taxes

With Social Security, as with everything, it is important to consider taxes. It may be surprising, but your Social Security benefits are not necessarily tax-free. Despite having been taxed to accrue those benefits in the first place, you may have to pay Uncle Sam income taxes on up to 85 percent of your Social Security.

---

[39] Social Security Administration. "Social Security Benefit Amounts For The Surviving Spouse By Year Of Birth."
https://www.ssa.gov/planners/survivors/survivorchartred.html

The Social Security Administration figures these taxes using what they call "the provisional income formula." Your provisional income formula differs from the adjusted gross income you use for your regular income taxes. Instead, to find out how much of your Social Security benefit is taxable, the Social Security Administration calculates it this way:

Provisional Income = Adjusted Gross Income + Nontaxable Interest + ½ of Social Security

See that piece about nontaxable interest? That generally means interest from government bonds and notes. It surprises many people that, although you may not pay taxes on those assets, their income will count against you when it comes to Social Security taxation.

Once you have figured out your provisional income (also called "combined income"), you can use the following chart to figure out your Social Security taxes.[40]

---

[40] Social Security Administration. "Benefits Planner: Income Taxes and Your Social Security Benefits." https://www.ssa.gov/planners/taxes.html

Taxes on Social Security		
Provisional Income = Adjusted Gross Income + Nontaxable Interest + ½ of Social Security		
If you are ____ and your provisional income is____, then...		Uncle Sam will tax ___ of your Social Security
Single	Married, filing jointly	
Less than $25,000	Less than $32,000	0%
$25,000 to $34,000	$32,000 to $44,000	Up to 50%
More than $34,000	More than $44,000	Up to 85%

This is one more reason it may benefit you to work with financial and tax professionals. They can look at your entire financial picture to make your overall retirement plan as tax-efficient as possible—including your Social Security benefit.

To reposition a couple to make their Social Security benefits more tax-efficient, I would show them that withdrawing less money from investments will reduce the tax on their Social Security by reducing their provisional income. They can have the same net amount of money and withdraw less from their nest egg.

Working and Social Security: The Earnings Test

If you haven't reached FRA, but you started your Social Security benefits and are still working, things get a little hairy.

Because you have started Social Security payments, the Social Security Administration will pay out your benefits (at that reduced rate, of course, because you haven't reached your

FRA). Yet, because you are working, the organization must also withhold from your check to add to your benefits, which you are already collecting. See how this complicates matters?

To address the situation, the government has what is called the earnings test. For 2022, you can earn up to $19,560 without it affecting your Social Security check. But, for every $2 you earn past that amount, the Social Security Administration will withhold $1. The earnings test loosens in the year of your FRA; if you are reaching FRA in 2022, you can earn up to $51,960 before you run into the earnings test, and the government only withholds $1 for every $3 past that amount. The month you reach FRA, you are no longer subject to any earnings withholding. For instance, if you are still working and will turn sixty-six on December 28, 2022, you would only have to worry about the earnings test until December, and then you can ignore it entirely. Keep in mind, the money the government withholds from your Social Security benefits while you are working before FRA will be tacked back onto your benefits check after FRA.[41]

Social Security planning with software can help to determine the right strategy, how much you need total, and what age you should consider taking Social Security.

---

[41] Social Security Administration. "Exempt Amounts Under the Earnings Test." https://www.ssa.gov/oact/cola/rtea.html

CHAPTER 11

401(k)s & IRAs

Have you heard? Today's retirement is not your parents' retirement. You see, back in the day, it was pretty common to work for one company for the vast majority of your career and then retire with a gold watch and a pension.

The gold watch was a symbol of the quality time you had put in at that company, but the pension was more than a symbol. Instead, it was a guarantee—as solid as your employer—that they would repay your hard work with a certain amount of income in your old age. Did you see the caveat there? Your pension's guarantee was *as solid as your employer*. The problem was, what if your employer went under?

Companies that failed couldn't pay their retired employees' pensions, leading to financial challenges for many. Beginning in 1974 with Congress' passage of the Employee Retirement Income Security Act, federal legislation and regulations aimed at protecting retirees were everywhere. One piece of legislation included a relatively obscure section of the Internal Revenue Code, added in 1978. Section 401(k), to be specific.

IRC section 401, subsection k, created tax advantages for employer-sponsored financial products, even if the main contributor was the employee him or herself. Over the years, more employers took note, beginning an age of transition away from pensions and toward 401(k) plans. A 401(k) is a retirement account with certain tax benefits and restrictions on the investments or other financial products inside of it.

Essentially, 401(k)s and their individual retirement account (IRA) counterparts are "wrappers" that provide tax benefits around assets; typically, the assets that compose IRAs and 401(k)s are mutual funds, stock and bond mixes, and money market accounts. However, IRA and 401(k) contents are becoming more diverse these days, with some companies offering different kinds of annuity options within their plans.

Where pensions are defined-*benefit* plans, 401(k)s and IRAs are defined-*contribution* plans. The one-word change outlines the basic difference. Pensions spell out what you can expect to receive from the plan but not necessarily how much money it will take to fund those benefits. With 401(k)s, an employer sets a standard for how much they will contribute (if any), and you can be certain of what you are contributing. Still, there is no outline for what you can expect to receive in return for those contributions.

Modern employment looks very different. A 2020 survey by the Bureau of Labor Statistics determined U.S. workers stayed with their employers a median of 4.1 years. Workers ages fifty-five to sixty-four had a little more staying power and were most likely to stay with their employer for about ten years.[42] Participation in 401(k) plans has steadily risen this century, totaling $7.3 trillion in assets in 2021 compared to $3.1 trillion in 2011. About 60 million active participants engaged in 401(k) plans in 2020.[43]

Those statistics make it clear that 401(k) plans have replaced pensions at many companies and, for that matter, a gold watch.

Very few private sector people have pensions, which is unfortunate because they go a long way toward providing what most people want when saving for retirement. The amount you save isn't as important as how much income you can derive

---

[42] Bureau of Labor Statistics. September 22, 2020. "Employee Tenure Summary." https://www.bls.gov/news.release/tenure.nr0.htm
[43] Investment Company Institute. October 11, 2021. "Frequently Asked Questions About 401(k) Plan Research." https://www.ici.org/faqs/faq/401k/faqs_401k

from what you save, and the pension skips right to the final step, giving you income that can be used once you retire.

If there is anything to learn from this paradigm shift, it's that you must look out for yourself. Whether you have worked for a company for two years or twenty, you are still the one who has to look out for your own best interests. That holds doubly true when it comes to preparing for retirement. If you are one of the lucky ones who still has a pension, good for you. But for the rest of us, it is likely a 401(k)—or possibly one of its nonprofit- or government-sector counterparts, a 403(b) or 457 plan—is one of your biggest assets for retirement.

Some employers offer incentives to contribute to their company plans, like a company match. On that subject, I have one thing to say: *Do it!* Nothing in life is free, as they say, but a company match on your retirement funds is about as close to free money as it gets. If you can make the minimum to qualify for your company's match at all, go for it.

Now, it's likely, during our working years, we mostly "set and forget" our 401(k) funding. Because it is tax-advantaged, your employer is taking money from your paycheck—before taxes—and putting it into your plan for you. Maybe you got to pick a selection of investments, or maybe your company only offers one choice of investment in your 401(k). Either way, while you are gainfully employed, your most impactful decision may just be the decision to continue funding your plan in the first place. But, when you are ready to retire or move jobs, you have choices to make requiring a little more thought and care.

When you are ready to part ways with your job, you have a few options:

- Leave the money where it is
- Take the cash (and pay income taxes and perhaps a 10 percent additional federal tax if you are younger than age fifty-nine-and-one-half)
- Transfer the money to another employer plan (if the new plan allows)
- Roll the money over into a self-directed IRA

Now, these are just general options. You will have to decide, hopefully with the help of a financial professional, what's right for you. For instance, 401(k)s are typically pretty closely tied to the companies offering them, so when changing jobs, it may not always be possible to transfer a 401(k) to another 401(k).

Also, remember what we mentioned earlier about how we change jobs more often these days? That means you likely have a 401(k) with your current company, but you may also have a string of retirement accounts trailing you from other jobs.

We have a client who was unaware of how much she had because she had so many different 401(k)s. When we work with clients, we take a big-picture look at all accounts so we can help determine where the client stands financially and the most efficient ways to use that money going forward. Once this client understood exactly how much money she had to work with, we were able to turn our attention to her goals in retirement and the path she could take to make them a reality.

When it comes to your retirement income, it's important to be able to pull together *all* your assets, so you can examine what you have and where, and then decide what you will do with it.

Tax-Qualified, Tax-Preferred, Tax-Deferred . . . Still TAXED

Financial media often cite IRAs and 401(k)s for their tax benefits. After all, with traditional plans, you put your money in, pre-tax, and it hopefully grows for years, even decades, untaxed. That's why these accounts are called "tax-qualified" or "tax-deferred" assets. They aren't *tax-free!* Rarely does Uncle Sam allow business to continue without receiving his piece of the pie, and your retirement assets are no different. If you didn't pay taxes on the front end, you will pay taxes on the money you withdraw from these accounts in retirement. Don't get me wrong: This isn't an inherently good or bad thing; it's just the way it is. It's important to understand, though, for the sake of planning ahead.

In retirement, many people assume they will be in a lower tax bracket. Are you planning to pare down your lifestyle in retirement? Perhaps you are, and perhaps you will have substantially less income in retirement. But many of my clients tell me they want to live life more or less the same as they always have. The money they would previously have spent on business attire or gas for their commute they now want to spend on hobbies and grandchildren. That's all fine, and for many of them, it is doable, but does it put them in a lower tax bracket? Probably not.

Keep in mind, IRAs, 401(k)s, and their alternatives have a few limitations because of their special tax status. For one thing, the IRS sets limits on your contributions to these retirement accounts. If you are contributing to a 401(k) or an equivalent nonprofit or government plan, your annual contribution limit is $20,500 (as of 2022). If you are fifty or older, the IRS allows additional contributions, called "catch-up contributions," of up to $6,500 on top of the regular limit of $20,500.[44] For an IRA, the limit is $7,000, with a catch-up limit of an additional $1,000.[45]

Because their tax advantages come from their intended use as retirement income, withdrawing funds from these accounts before you turn fifty-nine-and-one-half can carry stiff penalties. In addition to fees your investment management company might charge, you will have to pay income tax *and* a 10 percent federal tax penalty, with few exceptions.

The fifty-nine-and-one-half rule for retirement accounts is incredibly important to remember, especially when you're young. Younger workers are often tempted to cash out an IRA from a previous employer and then are surprised to find their checks missing 20 percent of the account value to income taxes, penalty taxes, and account fees.

---

[44] Jackie Stewart. Kiplinger.com. Dec. 17, 2021. "401(k) Contribution Limits for 2022" https://www.kiplinger.com/retirement/retirement-plans/401ks/603949/401k-contribution-limits-for-2022
[45] Fidelity.com. 2021. "IRA contribution limits."
https://www.fidelity.com/retirement-ira/contribution-limits-deadlines

Many millennials I see in my practice say, while they may be socking money away in their workplace retirement plan, it is often the *only* place they are saving. This could be problematic later because of the fifty-nine-and-one-half rule; what if you have an emergency? It is important to fund your retirement, but you need to have some liquid assets handy as emergency funds. This can help you avoid breaking into your retirement accounts and incurring taxes and penalties because of the fifty-nine-and-one-half rule.

RMDs

Remember how we talked about the 401(k) or IRA being a "tax wrapper" for your funds? Well, eventually, Uncle Sam will want a bite of that candy bar. So, when you turn seventy-two, the government requires you withdraw a portion of your account, which the IRS calculates based on the size of your account and your estimated lifespan. This required minimum distribution, or RMD, is the government's assurance it will collect some taxes, at some point, from your earnings. Because you didn't pay taxes on the front end, you will now pay income taxes on whatever you withdraw, including your RMDs. Also, let me just remind you not to play chicken with the U.S. government; if you don't take your RMDs starting at seventy-two, you will have to write a check to the IRS for *50 percent* of the amount of your missed RMDs. With the change in law from the SECURE Act of 2019, even after you begin RMDs, you can still also continue contributing to your 401(k) or IRAs if you are still employed, which can affect the whole discussion on RMDs and possible tax considerations.

If you don't need income from your retirement accounts, RMDs can seem like more of a tax burden than an income boon. While some people prefer to reinvest their RMDs, this comes with the possibility of additional taxation: You'll pay income taxes on your RMDs and then capital gains taxes on the growth of your investments. If you are legacy-minded, there are other ways to use RMDs, many of which have tax benefits.

Permanent Life Insurance

One way to turn those pesky RMDs into a legacy is through permanent life insurance. Assuming you need the death benefit coverage and can qualify for it medically, if properly structured, these products can pass on a sizeable death benefit to your beneficiaries, tax-free, as part of your general legacy plan.

ILIT

Another way to use RMDs toward your legacy is to work with an estate planning attorney to create an irrevocable life insurance trust (ILIT). This is basically a permanent life insurance policy placed within a trust. Because the trust is irrevocable, you would relinquish control of it, but, unlike with just a permanent life insurance policy, your death benefit won't count toward your taxable estate.

Annuities

Because annuities can be tax-deferred, using all or a portion of your RMDs to fund an annuity contract can be one way to further delay taxation while guaranteeing your income payments (either to you or your loved ones) later. (Assuming you don't need the RMD income during your retirement.)

Qualified Charitable Distributions

If you are charity-minded, you may use your RMDs toward a charitable organization instead of using them for income. You must do this directly from your retirement account (you can't take the RMD check and *then* pay the charity) for your withdrawals to be qualified charitable distributions (QCDs), but this is one way of realizing some of the benefits of a charitable legacy during your own lifetime. You will not need to pay taxes on your QCDs, and they won't count toward your annual charitable tax deduction limit, plus you'll be able to see how the organization you are supporting uses your donations. You should consult a financial professional on how to correctly make a QCD, particularly since the SECURE Act has implemented a few regulations on this point.[46]

Our preferred strategy for helping clients mitigate the tax consequences of RMDs is to go through a Roth conversion process, when appropriate, that shows clients scenario planning and how much they can Roth convert. At the end of the day, we believe this can be a great way to minimize the amount you must take out through RMDs.

Roth IRA

Since the Taxpayer Relief Act of 1997, there has been a different kind of retirement account, or "tax wrapper," available to the public: the Roth. Roth IRAs and Roth 401(k)s each differ from their traditional counterparts in one big way: You pay your taxes on the front end. This means, once your post-tax money is in the Roth account, as long as you follow the rules and limitations of that account, your distributions are truly tax-free. You won't pay income tax when you take withdrawals, so, in turn, you don't have to worry about RMDs. However, Roth accounts have the same limitations as traditional 401(k)s and IRAs when it comes to withdrawing money before age fifty-nine-and-one-half, with the added stipulation that the account must have been open for at least five years in order for the account holder to make withdrawals.

The first thing we do is determine what your RMD will be and figure out how that will affect you tax-wise. Then through scenario planning, we can show you how you may be able to Roth convert without causing your Medicare premiums to increase.

---

46 Bob Carlson. Forbes. January 28, 2020. "More Questions And Answers About The SECURE Act."
https://www.forbes.com/sites/bobcarlson/2020/01/28/more-questions-and-answers-about-the-secure-act/#113d49564869

Taking Charge

As mentioned earlier, the 401(k) and IRA have largely replaced pensions, but they aren't an equal trade.

Pensions are employer-funded; the money feeding into them is money that wouldn't ever show up on your pay stub. Because 401(k)s are self-funded, you must actively and consciously save. This distinction has made a difference when it comes to funding retirement. The average 401(k) balance for a person age sixty to sixty-nine is $198,600, but the median likely tells the full story. The median 401(k) balance for a person age sixty to sixty-nine is $62,000. A general suggestion derived from those statistics is to aim, by age thirty, to have saved an amount equal to 50 to 100 percent of your annual salary.[47] For some thirty-year-olds, saving half an annual salary by age thirty is more than some sixty-to-sixty-nine-year-olds have saved for their entire lives.

There can be many reasons why people underfund their retirement plans, like being overwhelmed by the investment choices or taking withdrawals from IRAs when they leave an employer. Still, the reason at the top of the list is this: People simply aren't participating to begin with.

So, whether you use a 401(k) with an employer or an IRA alternative with a private company, separate from your workplace, the most important retirement savings decision you can make is to sock away your money somewhere in the first place.

---

47 Arielle O'Shea. Nerd Wallet. March 17, 2021. "The Average 401(k) Balance by Age." https://www.nerdwallet.com/article/investing/the-average-401k-balance-by-age

CHAPTER 12

Annuities

In my practice, I offer my clients a variety of products—from securities to insurance—all designed to help them reach their financial goals. You may be wondering: Why single out a single product in this book?

Well, while most of my clients have a pretty good understanding of business and finance, I sometimes find those who have the impression there must be magic involved. Some people assume there is a magic finance wand we can wave to change years' worth of savings into a strategy for retirement income. But it's not as easy as a goose laying golden eggs or the Fairy Godmother turning a pumpkin into a coach!

Finances aren't magic; it takes lots of hard work and, typically, several financial products and strategies to pull together a complete retirement plan. Of all the financial products I work with, it seems people find none more mysterious than annuities. And, if I may say, even some of those who recognize the word "annuity" have a limited understanding of the product. So, in the interest of demystifying annuities, let me tell you a little about what an annuity is.

In general, insurance is a financial hedge against risk. Car owners buy auto insurance to protect their finances in case they injure someone or someone injures them. Homeowners have house insurance to protect their finances in case of a fire, flood, or another disaster. People have life insurance to protect their finances in case of untimely death. Almost juxtaposed to life insurance, people have annuities in case of a long life; annuities can give you financial protection by providing consistent and reliable income payments.

The basic premise of an annuity is you, the annuitant, pay an insurance company some amount in exchange for their contractual guarantee they will pay you income for a certain time period. How that company pays you, for how long, and how much they offer are all determined by the annuity contract you enter into with the insurance company.

How You Get Paid

There are two ways for an annuity contract to provide income: The first is through what is called annuitization, and the second is through the use of income riders. We'll get into income riders in a bit, but let's talk about annuitization. That nice, long word is, in my opinion, one reason annuities have a reputation for mystery and misinformation.

Annuitization

When someone "annuitizes" a contract, it is the point where he or she turns on the income stream. Once a contract has been annuitized, there is no going back. With annuities, if the policyholder lives longer than the insurance company planned, the insurance company is still obligated to pay him or her, even if the payments end up being way more than the contract's actual value. If, however, the policyholder dies an untimely death, depending on the contract type, the insurance company may keep anything left of the money that funded the annuity—nothing would be paid out to the contract holder's survivors. You see where that could make some people balk? Now, modern annuities rarely rely on annuitization for the income portion of the contract, and instead have so many bells and whistles that the old concept of annuitization seems outdated, but because this is still an option, it's important to at least understand the basic concept.

Riders

Speaking of bells and whistles, let's talk about riders. Modern annuities have a lot of different options these days, many in the form of riders you can add to your contract for a fee—usually about 1 percent of the contract value per year. Each rider has its particulars, and the types of riders available will vary by the type of annuity contract purchased, but I'll just briefly outline some of these little extras:

- Lifetime income rider: Contract guarantees you an enhanced income for life
- Death benefit rider: Contract pays an enhanced death benefit to your beneficiaries even if you have annuitized
- Return of premium rider: Guarantees you (or your beneficiaries) will at least receive back the premium value of the annuity
- Long-term care rider: Provides a certain amount, sometimes as much as twice the principal value of the contract, or it may double your income payments for a period of time, to help pay for long-term care if the contract holder is moved to a nursing home or assisted living situation

This isn't an extensive look, and usually the riders have fancier names based on the issuing company, like "Lorem Ipsum Insurance Company Income Preferred Bonus Fixed Index Annuity rider," but I just wanted to show you what some of the general options are in layperson's terms.

Types of Annuities

Annuities break down into four basic types: immediate, variable, fixed, and fixed index.

Immediate

Immediate annuities primarily rely on annuitization to provide income—you give the insurance company a lump sum up front, and your payments begin immediately. Once you begin receiving income payments, the transaction is irreversible, and you no longer have access to your money in a lump sum. When you die, any remaining contract value is typically forfeited to the insurance company.

All other annuity contract types are "deferred" contracts, meaning you fund your policy as a lump sum or over a period of years and you give it the opportunity to grow over time—sometimes years, sometimes decades.

Variable

A variable annuity is an insurance contract as well as an investment. It's sold by insurance companies, but only through someone who is registered to sell investment products. With a variable annuity contract, the insurance company invests your premiums in subaccounts that are tied to the stock market. This makes it a bit different from the other annuity contract types because it is the only contract where your money is subject to losses because of market declines. Your contract value has a greater opportunity to grow, but it also stands to lose. Additionally, your contract's value will be subject to the underlying investment's fees and limitations—including capital gains taxes, management fees, etc. Once it is time for you to receive income from the contract, the insurance company will pay you a certain income, locked in at whatever your contract's value was.

Fixed

A traditional fixed annuity is pretty straightforward. You purchase a contract with a guaranteed interest rate and, when you are ready, the insurance company will make regular income payments to you at whatever payout rate your contract guarantees. Those payments will continue for the rest of your life and, if you choose, for the remainder of your spouse's life.

Fixed annuities don't have much in the way of upside potential, but many people like them for their guarantees (after all, if your Aunt May lives to be ninety-five, knowing she has a paycheck later in life can be her mental and financial safety net), as well as for their predictability. Unlike variable annuities, which are subject to market risk and might be up one year and down the next, you can easily calculate the value of your fixed annuity over your lifetime.

Fixed Index

To recap, variable annuities take on more risk to offer more possibilities to grow. Fixed annuities have less potential growth, but they protect your principal. In the last couple of decades, many insurance companies have retooled their product line to offer fixed index annuities, which are sort of midway between variable and fixed annuities on that risk/reward spectrum. Fixed index annuities offer greater growth potential than traditional fixed annuities but less than variable annuities. Like traditional fixed annuities, however, fixed index annuities are protected from downside market losses.

Fixed index annuities earn interest that is tied to the market, meaning that, instead of your contract value growing at a set interest rate like a traditional fixed annuity, it has the potential to grow within a range. Your contract's value is credited interest based on the performance of an external market index like the S&P 500 while never being invested in the market itself. You can't invest in the S&P 500 directly, but each year, your annuity as the potential to earn interest based on the chosen index's performance, submit to limits set by the company such as caps, spreads and participation rates. For instance, if your contract caps your interest at 5 percent, then in a year that the S&P 500 gains 3 percent, your annuity value increases 3 percent. If the S&P 500 gains 35 percent, your annuity value gets a 5 percent interest bump. But since your money isn't actually invested in the market with a fixed index annuity, if the market nosedives (such as happened during 2000, 2008 and 2020, anyone?) you won't see any increase in your contract value. Conversely, there will also be no decrease in your contract value—no matter how badly the market performed, as long as you follow the terms of the contract, you won't lose any of the interest you were credited in previous years.

So, what if the S&P 500 shows a market loss of 30 percent? Your contract value isn't going anywhere (unless you purchased an optional rider—this charge will still come out of your annuity value each year). For those who are more interested in protection than growth potential, fixed index annuities can be an attractive option because, when the stock market has a long period of positive performance, a fixed index annuity can enjoy conservative growth. And, during stretches where the stock market is erratic and stock values across the board take significant losses? Fixed index annuities won't lose anything due to the stock market volatility.

We go through a reallocation process where the person tells us how much they want to keep protected. We are agnostic toward annuities. I've had some clients say they don't want any risk, and when it comes to protected-money financial vehicles, FIAs can be attractive options.

On the other hand, I have had clients say they don't like annuities. I don't push one way or the other—everyone's situation is different.

Other Things to Know About Annuities

We just talked about the four kinds of annuity contracts available, but all of them have some commonalities as annuities.

For all annuities, the contractual guarantees are only as strong as the insurance company that sells the product, which makes it important to thoroughly check the credit ratings of any company whose products you are considering.

Annuities are tax-deferred, meaning you don't have to pay taxes on interest earnings each year as the contract value grows. Instead, you will pay ordinary income taxes on your withdrawals. These are meant to be long-term products, so, like other tax-deferred or tax-advantaged products, if you begin taking withdrawals from your contract before age fifty-nine-and-one-half, you may also have to pay a 10 percent federal tax penalty. Also, while annuities are generally considered illiquid, most contracts allow you to withdraw up to 10 percent of your contract value every year. Withdraw any more, however, and you could incur additional surrender penalties.

Keep in mind, your withdrawals will deplete the accumulated cash value, death benefit, and, possibly, the rider values of your contract.

I had a business owner come in one time. He said he had all the risk he needed in his business, and all the money he had with us he wanted protected, so he did through the use of an FIA.

Annuities aren't for everyone, but it's important to understand them before saying "yea" or "nay" on whether they fit into your plan; otherwise, you're not operating with complete information, wouldn't you agree? Regardless, you should talk to a financial professional who can help you understand annuities, help you dissect your particular financial needs, and help show you whether an annuity is appropriate for your retirement income plan.

CHAPTER 13

Estate & Legacy

In my practice, I devote a significant portion of my time to matters of estates. That doesn't mean drawing up wills or trusts or putting together powers of attorney or anything like that. After all, I'm not an estate planning attorney. But I am a financial professional, and what part of the "estate" isn't affected by money matters?

I've included this chapter because I have seen many people do estate planning wrong. Clients, or clients' families, have come in after experiencing a death in the family and have found themselves in the middle of probate, high taxes, or a discovery of something unforeseen draining the estate.

I have also seen people do estate planning right: clients or families who visit my office to talk about legacies and how to make them last and adult children who have room to grieve without an added burden of unintended costs, without stress from a family ruptured because of inadequate planning.

I'll share some of these stories here. However, I'm not going to give you specific advice, since everyone's situation is unique. I only want to give you some things to think about and to underscore the importance of planning ahead.

You Can't Take It With You

When it comes to legacy and estate planning, the most important thing is to *do it*. I have heard people from clients to

115

celebrities (rap artist Snoop Dogg comes to mind) say they aren't interested in what happens to their assets when they die because they'll be dead. That's certainly one way to look at it. But I think that's a very selfish way to go about things—we all have people and causes we care about, and those who care about us. Even if the people we love don't *need* what we leave behind, they can still be fined or legally tied up in the probate process or burial costs if we don't plan for those. And that's not even considering what happens if you become incapacitated at some point while you are still alive. Having a plan in place can greatly reduce the stress of those responsibilities on your loved ones; it's just a loving thing to do.

Documents

There are a few documents that lay the groundwork of legacy planning. You've probably heard of all or most of them, but I'd like to review what they are and how people commonly use them. These are all things you should talk about with an estate planning attorney to establish your legacy.

Powers of Attorney

A power of attorney, or POA, is a document giving someone the authority to act on your behalf and in your best interests. These come in handy in situations where you cannot be present (think a vacation where you get stuck in Canada) or, for durable powers of attorney, even when you are incapacitated (think in a coma or coping with dementia).

It is important to have powers of attorney in place and to appoint someone you trust to act on your behalf in these matters. Have you ever heard of someone who was incapacitated after a car accident, whether from head trauma or being in a coma for weeks—sometimes months? Do you think their bills stopped coming due during that time? I like my phone company and my bank, but neither one is about to put a moratorium on sending me bills, particularly not for an extended or interminable period. A power of attorney would have the authority to pay your mortgage or cancel your cable while you are unable.

You can have multiple POAs and require them to act jointly.

What this looks like: Do you think two heads are better than one? One man, Chris, significantly relied on his two sons' opinions for both his business and personal matters. He appointed both sons as joint POA, requiring both their signoffs for his medical and financial matters.

You can have multiple POAs who can act independently.

What this looks like: Irene had three children with whom she routinely stayed. They lived in different areas of the country, which she thought was an advantage; one month she might be hiking out West, the next she could enjoy the newest off-Broadway production, and the next she could soak up some Southern sun. She named her three children as independently authorized POAs, so, if something happened, no matter where she was, the child closest could step in to act on her behalf.

You can have POAs who have different responsibilities.

What this looks like: Although Luke's friend Claire, a nurse, was his go-to and POA for health-related issues, financial matters usually made her nervous, so he appointed his good neighbor, Matt, as his POA in all of his financial and legal matters.

In addition to POAs, it may be helpful to have an advanced medical directive. This is a document where you have pre-decided what choices you would make about different health scenarios. An advanced medical directive can help ease the burden for your medical POA and loved ones, particularly when it comes to end-of-life care.

We had a couple come into our office to meet us after attending one of our estate planning presentations, and they realized they needed a POA. However, they both had dementia, and because of this, when the husband went into a nursing home, the wife could not access his assets and had they had to go through conservatorship.

Wills

Perhaps the most basic document of legacy planning, a will is a legal document wherein you outline your wishes for your estate. When it comes to your estate after your death, having a will is the foundation of your legacy. Without one, your loved ones are left behind, guessing what you would have wanted, and the court will likely split your assets according to the state's defaults. Maybe that's exactly what you wanted, as far as anyone knows, right? Because even if you told your nephew he could have your car he's been driving, if it's not in writing, it still might go to the brother, sister, son, or daughter to whom you aren't speaking.

However, it may not be enough just to have a will. Even with a will, your assets will be subject to probate. Probate is what we call the state's process for determining a will's validity. A judge will go through your will to question if it conflicts with state law, if it is the most up-to-date document, if you were mentally competent at the time it was in order, etc. For some, this is a quick, easily-resolved process. For others, particularly if someone steps forward to contest the will, it may take years to settle, all the while subjecting the assets to court costs and attorney's fees.

One other undesirable piece of the probate process is that it is a public process. That means anyone can go to the courthouse, ask for copies of the case, and discover your assets. They can also see who is slated to receive what and who is disputing.

It's also important to remember beneficiary lines trump wills. So, that large life insurance policy? What if, when you bought it fifteen years ago, you wrote your ex-husband's name on the beneficiary line? Even if you stipulate otherwise in your will, the company that holds your policy will pay out to your ex-spouse. Or, how about the thousands of dollars in your IRA you dedicated to the children thirty years ago, but one of your children was killed in a car accident, leaving his wife and two toddlers behind? That IRA is going to transfer to your remaining children, with nothing for your daughter-in-law and grandchildren.

That may paint a grim portrait, but I can't underscore enough the importance of working with a skilled estate planning attorney to keep your will and beneficiary lines up to date as your life changes.

There are several movie stars and singers who didn't have an estate plan or didn't fund their estate plan, including Elvis, Aretha Franklin, Prince, and Micheal Jackson. On a personal level, I watched my wife grieve as she had to make medical decisions for her aging mother because her mother did not have a health care directive.

Trusts

Another piece of legacy planning to consider is the trust.

A trust is set up through an attorney and allows a third party, or trustee, to hold your assets and determine how they will pass to your beneficiaries. Many people are skeptical of trusts because they assume trusts are only appropriate for the fabulously wealthy.

However, a simple trust will likely cost more than $1,000 if prepared by an attorney and fees can be higher for couples.[48] But a trust can help you avoid both the expense and publicity of probate, provide a more immediate transfer of wealth, avoid some taxes, and provide you greater control over your legacy.

---

[48] Rickie Houston. smartasset.com. "How Much Does It Cost to Set Up a Trust? https://smartasset.com/estate-planning/how-much-does-it-cost-to-set-up-a-trust

For instance, if you want to set aside some funds for a grandchild's college education, you can make it a requirement he or she enrolls in classes before your trust will dispense any funds. Like a will, beneficiary lines will override your trust conditions, so you must still keep insurance policies and other assets up to date.

Like any financial or legal consideration, there are many options these days beyond the simple "yes or no" question of whether to have a trust. For one thing, you will need to consider if you want your trust to be revocable (you can change the terms while you are alive) or irrevocable (can't be changed; you are no longer the "owner" of the contents). A brief note here about irrevocable trusts: Although they have significant and greater tax benefits, they are still subject to a Medicaid look-back period. This means, if you transfer your assets into an irrevocable trust in an attempt to shelter them from a Medicaid spend-down, you will be ineligible for Medicaid coverage of long-term care for five years. Yet, an irrevocable trust can avoid both probate and estate taxes, and it can even protect assets from legal judgments against you.

Another thing to remember when it comes to trusts, in general, is, even if you have set up a trust, you must remember to fund it. In my thirty-five years' of work, I've had numerous clients come to me, assuming they have protected their assets with a trust. When we talk about taxes and other pieces of their legacy, it turns out they never retitled any assets or changed any paperwork on the assets they wanted in the trust. So, please remember, a trust is just a bunch of fancy legal papers if you haven't followed through on retitling your assets.

Taxes

Although charitable contributions, trusts, and other tax-efficient strategies can reduce your tax bill, it's unlikely your estate will be passed on entirely tax-free. Yet, when it comes to building a legacy that can last for generations, taxes can be one of the heaviest drains on the impact of your hard work.

For 2020, the federal estate exemption was $11.58 million per individual and $23.16 million for a married couple, with estates facing up to a 40 percent tax rate after that. In 2022, those limits increased to $12.06 million for individuals and $24.12 million for married couples, with the 40 percent top level gift and estate tax remaining the same. Currently, the new estate limits are set to increase with inflation until January 1, 2026, when they will "sunset" back to the inflation-adjusted 2017 limits.[49] And that's not taking into account the various state regulations and taxes regarding estate and inheritance transfers.

Another tax concern "frequent flyer": retirement accounts.

Your IRA or 401(k) can be a source of tax issues when you pass away. For one thing, taking funds from a sizeable account can trigger a large tax bill. However, if you leave the assets in the account, there are still required minimum distributions (RMDs), which will take effect even after you die. If you pass the account to your spouse, he or she can keep taking your RMDs as is, or your spouse can retitle the account in his or her name and receive RMDs based on his or her life expectancy. Remember, if you don't take your RMDs, the IRS will take up to 50 percent of whatever your required distribution was, plus you will still have to pay income taxes whenever you withdraw that money. Thanks to the enactment of the SECURE Act, anyone who inherits your IRA, with few exceptions (your spouse, a beneficiary less than ten years younger, or a disabled adult child, to name a few), will need to empty the account within ten years of your death.[50]

Also—and this is a pretty big also—check with an attorney if you are considering putting your IRA or 401(k) in a trust. An improperly titled beneficiary form for the IRA could mean the

---

[49] Laura Sanders, Richard Rubin. The Wall Street Journal. March 10, 2022. "Estate and Gift Taxes 2021-2022: "What's New This Year and What You Need to Know." https://www.wsj.com/articles/estate-and-gift-taxes-what-to-know-2021-2022-11646426764
[50] Julia Kagan. Investopedia. October 11, 2020. "Stretch IRA." https://www.investopedia.com/terms/s/stretch-ira.asp

difference of thousands of dollars in taxes. This is just one more reason to work with a financial professional, one who can strategically partner with an estate planning attorney to diligently check your decisions.

CHAPTER 14

Women Retire Too

I help men, women, and families from all walks of life on their journey to and through retirement. Yet, I want to address the female demographic specifically. Why? To be perfectly blunt, women are more likely to deal with poverty than men when they reach retirement. One report notes that of the people living in poverty in the U.S., 56 percent are women.[51]

The topics, products, and strategies I cover elsewhere in this book are meant to help address retirement concerns for men *and* women, but the dire statistic above is a reminder that much of traditional planning is geared toward men. Male careers, male lifespans, male health care. The bottom line is women's career paths often look much different than men's, so why would their retirement planning look the same?

Women often embrace different roles and values than men as workers, wives, mothers, and daughters. They are more apt to take on roles as caretakers. They often plan for events, worry about loved ones, tend to details, and think about the future. Also, they often want everything to be just right, and they want to be right themselves. It could be you've seen the following affixed to a decorative sign, refrigerator magnet, or T-shirt: "If

---

[51] Robin Bleiweis, Diana Boesch. Center for American Progress. August 3, 2020. "The Basic Facts About Women in Poverty."
https://www.americanprogress.org/issues/women/reports/2020/08/03/488536/basic-facts-women-poverty

I agreed with you, we'd both be wrong." The barb features a picture of a woman speaking to a man.

If these characteristics I listed about women are accurate, shouldn't they deserve special considerations from financial professionals? The case can be made, particularly since 70 percent of men in the U.S. age 65 and older happen to be married, compared to 47 percent of women in that age classification.[52] Single women don't have the opportunity to capitalize on the resource pooling and economies of scale accompanying a marriage or partnership.

Women-specific concerns should be addressed separately because women generally live longer than men, and there's a solid chance they could outlive their money. My own mother outlived her money, and in watching what she went through, I don't want to see any of our clients go through that.

Be Informed

It's a familiar scene in many financial offices across the country: A woman comes into an appointment carrying a sack full of unopened envelopes. Often through tears, she sits across the desk from a financial professional and apologizes her way through a conversation about what financial products she owns and where her income is coming from. She is recently widowed and was sure her spouse was taking care of the finances, but now she doesn't know where all their assets are kept, and her confidence in her financial outlook has wavered after walking through funeral expenses and realizing she's down to one income.

Often, she may be financially "okay." Yet, the uncertainty can be wearying, particularly when the family is already reeling from a loss. While this scenario sometimes plays out with men, in my experience, it's more likely to be a woman in that chair

---

[52] Administration for Community Living. May 27, 2021. "Profile of Older Americans." https://acl.gov/aging-and-disability-in-america/data-and-research/profile-older-americans

across from my desk, probably, in part, because of Western traditions about money management being "a guy thing." But it doesn't have to be this way. This all-too-common scenario can be wiped away with just a little preparation.

Talk to Your Spouse/ Work with a Financial Professional

While there are many factors affecting women's financial preparation for and situation in retirement, I cannot emphasize enough that the decision to be informed, to be a part of the conversation, and to be aware of what is going on with your finances is absolutely paramount to a confident retirement. With all the couples I've seen, there is almost always an "alpha" when it comes to finances. It isn't always men—for many of my coupled clients, the wife is the alpha who keeps the books and budgets and knows where all of the family's assets are, down to the penny—yet, statistically, among baby boomers it is usually a man who runs the books. But, as time goes on, it looks like the ratio of male to female financial alphas is evening out. According to a Gallup study, women are equally as likely to take the lead on finances as men, with 37 percent of U.S. households showing women primarily paying the bills. Half of households also say decisions about savings and investments are shared equally.[53] Whether that's the way your household works or not, there isn't anything wrong with who does what.

The breakdown happens when there is a lack of communication, when no one other than the financial alpha knows how much the family has and where. In the end, it doesn't matter who handles the money; it's about all parties being informed of what's going on financially.

There are a lot of ways to open the conversation about money. One woman started a conversation with her husband,

---

[53] Megan Brenan. Gallup. January 29, 2020. "Women Still Handle Main Household Tasks in U.S." https://news.gallup.com/poll/283979/women-handle-main-household-tasks.aspx

the financial alpha, by sitting down and saying, "Teach me how to be a widow." Perhaps that sounds grim, but it was to the point, and it spurred what she said was a very fruitful conversation. Couples sometimes have their first real conversation about money, assets, and their retirement income approach, in our office. The important thing about having these conversations isn't where, it's when . . . and the best "when" is as soon as possible.

A woman once commented to me that to get this conversation rolling, she asked her husband "to teach her how to be a widow." They spent a day, just one part of an otherwise dull weekend, going through everything she might need to know. They spent the better part of two decades together after that. When he died, and she was widowed, she said the "widowhood" talk had made a huge difference. She knew who to call to talk through their retirement plan and where to call for the insurance policy.

She said the fruit of the weekend exercise they engaged in some twenty years earlier couldn't have been more apparent than when she ultimately accompanied a recently widowed friend of hers to a financial appointment. Her friend was emotional the whole time, afraid she would run out of money any day. The financial professional ultimately showed the friend that she was financially in good shape, but not before the friend had already spent months worried that each check would exhaust her bank account. That's no way to live after losing a loved one. It was preventable had her deceased spouse and financial professional included her in a conversation about "widowhood."

Spouse-Specific Options

One area where it might be especially important to be on the same page between spouses is when it comes to financial products or services that have spousal options. A few that come to mind are pensions and Social Security, although life insurance and annuity policies also have the potential to affect both spouses.

With pensions, taking the worker's life-only option is somewhat attractive—after all, the monthly payment is bigger. However, you and your spouse should discuss your options. When we're talking about both of you, as opposed to just one lifespan, there is an increased likelihood at least one of you will live a long, long time. This means the monthly payout will be less, but it also ensures that, no matter which spouse outlives the other, no one will have to suffer the loss of a needed pension paycheck in his or her later retirement years.

While we covered Social Security options in chapter five, I think some of the spousal information bears repeating. Particularly, if you worked exclusively inside the home for a significant number of years, you may want to talk about taking your Social Security benefits based on your spouse's work history. After all, Social Security is based on your thirty-five highest-earning years.

Things to remember about the spousal benefits:[54]

- Your benefit will be calculated as a percentage (up to 50 percent) of your spouse's earned monthly benefit at his or her full retirement age, or FRA.

- For you to begin receiving a spousal benefit, your spouse must have already filed for his or her own benefits and you must be at least sixty-two.

- You can qualify for a full half of your spouse's benefits if you wait until you reach FRA to file.

- Beginning your benefits earlier than your FRA will reduce your monthly check but waiting to file until after FRA will not increase your benefits.

---

[54] Social Security Administration. "Retirement Planner: Benefits For You As A Spouse." https://www.ssa.gov/planners/retire/applying6.html

For divorcees:[55]

- You may qualify for an ex-spousal benefit if . . .
    a. You were married for a decade or more
    b. **and** you are at least sixty-two
    c. **and** you have been divorced for at least two years
    d. **and** you are currently unmarried
    e. **and** your ex-spouse is sixty-two (qualifies to begin taking Social Security)
- Your ex-spouse does not need to have filed for you to file on his or her benefit.
- Similar to spousal benefits, you can qualify for up to half of your ex-spouse's benefits if you wait to file until your FRA.
- If your ex-spouse dies, you may file to receive a widow/widower benefit on his or her Social Security record as long as you are at least age sixty and fulfill all the other requirements on the preceding alphabetized list.
    a. This will not affect the benefits of your ex-spouse's current spouse

For widow's (or widower's, for that matter) benefits:[56]

- You may qualify to receive as much as your deceased spouse would have received if . . .
    a. You were married for at least nine months before his or her death
    b. **or** you would qualify for a divorced spousal benefit
    c. **and** you are at least sixty
    d. **and** you did not/have not remarried before age sixty

---

[55] Social Security Administration. "Retirement Planner: If You Are Divorced." https://www.ssa.gov/planners/retire/divspouse.html
[56] Social Security Administration. "Survivors Planner: If You Are The Worker's Widow Or Widower." https://www.ssa.gov/planners/survivors/ifyou.html#h2

- You may earn delayed credits on your spouse's benefit *if* your spouse hadn't already filed for benefits when he or she died.
- Other rules may apply to you if you are disabled or are caring for a deceased spouse's dependent or disabled child.

Longevity

On average, women live longer than men. Most stats put average female longevity at about two years more than men. But averages are tricky things. An April 2022 report by the World Economic Forum listed the eight oldest people in the world to all be women. They ranged in age from 118 years old to 114 and included two Americans.[57]

On one hand, this is a Brandi Chastain moment. You know, when the American soccer icon shed her jersey to celebrate a game-winning penalty kick to win the World Cup. Seriously, how fabulous are women? They tend to be meticulous, resolute, perseverant. On the other hand, the trend for women to live longer presents longstanding financial ramifications.

Simply Needing More Money in Retirement

Living longer in retirement means needing more money, period. Barring a huge lottery win or some crazy stock market action, the date you retire is likely the point at which you have the most money you will ever have. Not to put too grim a spin on it, but the problem with longevity is, the further you get away

---

[57] Martin Armstrong. World Economic Forum. April 29, 2022. "How old are the world's oldest people?"
https://www.weforum.org/agenda/2022/04/the-oldest-people-in-the-world

from that date, the further your dollars have to stretch. If you planned to live to a nice eighty-something but live to a nice one-hundred-something, that is *two decades* you will need to account for, monetarily.

To put this in perspective, let's say you like to drink coffee as an everyday splurge. Not accounting for inflation or leap years, a $2.50 cup-a-day habit is $18,250 over a two-decade span. Now, think of all the things you like to do that cost money. Add those up for twenty years of unanticipated costs. I think you'll see what I mean.

During the 2020 onset of the coronavirus pandemic, many learned to cut costs. For some, that amounted to skipping their decadent latte. For others, however, cutbacks became acute. According to data compiled by Age Wave and Edward Jones, 32 percent of Americans plan to retire later than planned because of the pandemic. Women felt a more adverse effect. The report stipulated that 41 percent of women continued to save for retirement, compared to 58 percent of men.[58]

More Health Care Needs

In addition to the cost of living for a longer lifespan is the fact aging, plain and simple, means more health care, and more health care means more money. Women are survivors. They suffer from the morbidity-mortality paradox, which states women suffer more non-fatal illnesses throughout their lifetime than men, who experience fewer illnesses but higher mortality.

Women have been found to seek treatment more often when not feeling well and emphasize staying healthy when older,

---

[58] Megan Leonhardt. cnbc.com. June 16, 2021. "58% of men were able to continue saving for retirement during the pandemic—but only 41% of women were." https://www.cnbc.com/2021/06/16/why-pandemic-hit-womens-retirement-savings-more-than-mens.html

according to studies.[59] So survival is on the side of the woman. However, surviving things, like cancer, also means more checkups later in life.

Widowhood

Not only do women typically live longer than their same-age male counterparts, they also have the tendency to marry men older than themselves. The numbers bear this out: Worldwide, one in five women live in a solo household after turning sixty compared to one in ten men.[60]

I don't write this to scare people; rather, I think it's fundamentally important to prepare my female clients for something that may be a startling, *but very likely,* scenario. At some point, most women will have to handle their financial situations on their own. A little preparation can go a long way, and having a basic understanding of your household finances and the "who, what, where, and how much" of your family's assets is incredibly useful—it can prevent a tragic situation from being more traumatic.

In my opinion, the financial services industry sometimes underserves women in these situations. Some financial professionals tend to alienate women, even when their spouses are alive. I've heard several stories of women who sat through meeting after meeting without their financial professional ever addressing a single question to them.

In our firm, when we work with couples, we work hard to make sure our retirement income strategies work for *both* people. No matter who the financial alpha is, it's important for everyone affected by a retirement strategy to understand it.

---

[59] advisory.com. July 22, 2020. "Why do women live longer than men? It's more complicated than you think." https://www.advisory.com/en/daily-briefing/2020/07/22/longevity
[60] Jacob Ausubel. Pew Research Center. January 3, 2020. "Globally, women are younger than their male partners, more likely to age alone" https://www.pewresearch.org/fact-tank/2020/01/03/globally-women-are-younger-than-their-male-partners-more-likely-to-age-alone

Many of our clients are widowed. There's a great chance other women will outlive their spouses, so having proper long-term care needs covered is critical.

Taxes

One of the often-unexpected aspects of widowhood is the tax bill. Many women continue similar lifestyles to the ones they shared with their spouses. This, in turn, means continuing to have a similar need for income. However, after the death of a spouse, their taxes will be calculated based on a single filer's income table, which is much less forgiving than the couple's tax rates. With proper planning, your financial professional and tax advisor may be able to help you take the sting out of your new tax status.

Caregiving

Of the 53 million caregivers providing unpaid, informal care for older adults in 2020, 61 percent are women. Among today's family caregivers, 61 percent work and 45 percent report some kind of financial impact from providing a loved one care and support.[61] In addition to the financial burden created by caregiving responsibilities, women devote an average of 5.7 hours each day to duties such as housekeeping and looking after loved ones. [62] So then, when can women find the time to focus long and hard on financial matters?

Unfortunately, the impact and hardships created by traditional roles for women typically do not account for Social Security benefit losses or the losses of health care benefits and retirement savings. This also doesn't account for maternity

---

[61] caregiving.org. 2020 Report. "Caregiving in the U.S. 2020."
https://www.caregiving.org/caregiving-in-the-us-2020
[62] Drew Weisholtz. Today. January 22, 2020. "Women do 2 more hours of housework daily than men, study says."
https://www.today.com/news/women-do-2-more-hours-housework-daily-men-study-says-t172272

care, mothers who homeschool, or women who leave the workforce to care for their children in any way.

I don't repeat these statistics to scare you. Not only are unpaid family caregivers spending their time and energy taking care of others, but they're also putting their own money towards the cause. An AARP study found that three-quarters of family caregivers surveyed were spending an average of $7,242 a year on out-of-pocket caregiving costs.[63] Yet, I think the emotional value of the care many women provide their elderly relatives or neighbors cannot be quantified. So, to be clear, this shouldn't be taken as a "why not to provide caregiving" spiel. Instead, it should be seen as a call for "why to *prepare* for caregiving" or "how to lessen the financial and emotional burden of caregiving."

Funding Your Own Retirement

For these reasons, women need to be prepared to fund more of their own retirements. There are several savings options and products, including the spousal 401(k). Unlike a traditional 401(k), where you contribute money to a plan with your employer, a spousal 401(k) is something your spouse sets up on your behalf, so he or she can contribute a portion of the paycheck to your retirement funds. This is something to consider, particularly for families where one spouse has dropped out of the workforce to care for a relative.

Also, if you find yourself in a caregiving role, talk to your employer's human resources department. Some companies have paid leave, special circumstance, or sick leave options you could qualify for, making it easier to cope and helping you stay in the workforce longer.

---

[63] Nancy Kerr. AARP. June 29, 2021. " Family Caregivers Spend More Than $7,200 a Year on Out-of-Pocket Costs."
https://www.aarp.org/caregiving/financial-legal/info-2021/high-out-of-pocket-costs.html

Saving Money

Women need more money to fund their retirements, period. But this doesn't have to be a significant burden—most of the time, women are better at saving, while usually taking less risk in their portfolios.[64] This gives me reason to believe, as women get more involved in their finances, families will continue to be better-prepared for retirement, both *his* and *hers*.

---

[64] Maurie Backman. The Motley Fool. March 4, 2021. "A Summary of 20 Years of Research and Statistics on Women in Investing." https://www.fool.com/research/women-in-investing-research

CHAPTER 15

Charity

Wills and testaments, trusts and powers of attorney—these are all pieces of what we often call legacy planning. But I would be remiss if I didn't address a piece of legacy preparation near and dear to my heart: charitable contributions.

Charity is one of those universal concepts that unites us as human beings. Football players who dedicate their resources to building homes for single moms, communities who help neighbors rebuild after catastrophes, groundskeepers who donate millions from under a mattress to their favorite university, or private donors who put impoverished children through school. . .these are the stories that inspire us, that drive us to be better people.

There are many, many ways to pass money to your favorite charity, university, foundation, or public resource. Some include using qualified charitable distributions with the mandatory withdrawals from your IRA, and others lend themselves to establishing trusts. Whatever your preferred method of charitable distribution, the right financial professional will partner with a qualified tax advisor and/or estate planning attorney to discover how to help you make your contributions in a way that fits well within your own strategy for taxes—helping to ensure your contributions are passed efficiently to your intended beneficiary.

We, as a company, support ten different missions. We believe strongly in giving back, and a picture of each mission is in the foyer of our lobby. Among the community causes we support are: City Union Mission, Parkville women's clinic, Oak Tree Church, The Calling Community Church, Crossworld, and Rocsanna's Hope.

Where to Start?

We've all heard it is better to give than to receive, and science backs this up. Multiple studies show those who give to charity or volunteer experience less depression, lower blood pressure, higher self-esteem, and greater happiness.[65]

It's a common perception, however, that retirees are less inclined to be charitable. It seems like reasoned logic—they're living on fixed incomes, and it's difficult to work charitable giving into conservative strategies designed to protect assets. But this counters the facts. In 2021, more baby boomers donated to charities than any other generations.[66]

So, how do we keep up—or even increase—our donations in retirement? Well, as with all the other topics we cover in this book, step one is to build charitable giving into our retirement plans. Advanced planning can help you be sure your donations—at least in the monetary sense—are given a tax-efficient and effective way, both for you and for the charity to which you are contributing.

---

[65] "Volunteering and Its Surprising Benefits."
https://www.helpguide.org/articles/healthy-living/volunteering-and-its-surprising-benefits.htm
[66] Dawn Papandrea. Lendingtree. November 29, 2021. "56% of Americans Donated to Charity in 2021, at Average of $574."
https://www.lendingtree.com/debt-consolidation/charitable-donations-survey-study

Planned Giving: Lifetime

When we're talking about charitable contributions, it's important to distinguish between lifetime giving and charitable giving as part of a well-prepared estate plan.

The American tax system has many provisions to encourage charitable giving. I'm sure the reasoning goes something along the lines of, if we the people were naturally able, through our own means, to care for the poor and vulnerable in our own communities, we collectively would need to pay fewer taxes to support federal aid to those same people. It's a wonderful consideration, and one we should all aspire to. But, in practice, it gets more difficult, as tax codes change and shift according to political administrations and other public considerations. Ensuring your charitable contributions are tax-efficient is not a one-time move—it requires yearly analysis.

It's important to remember your charitable giving is usually most effective when the combined amount of your *itemized* deductions is more than your *standard* deduction. Now it isn't only charity that counts toward your itemized deduction; there are also homeowner and business owner credits, adoption credits, etc. But, as it pertains to charity, if you haven't contributed a significant amount to charity in a certain tax year, it may not be worth counting on your taxes.

Deductions change year-to-year, of course, but the IRS usually publishes the following year's charts in November. When you're itemizing deductions, you may deduct up to 50 percent of your adjusted gross (pre-tax) income, with a few exceptions.

Another thing to keep in mind if you are considering the tax implications of a charitable donation, you must have a receipt, a canceled check, or some demonstrable way of recording the transaction. Additionally, many charitable activities aren't eligible for tax credits. Raffle tickets, charity event entrance fees, and those sorts of things are not typically counted as charitable deductions on your taxes—a quick rule of thumb is, if you received something in return for your donation, it's not tax-deductible.

Perhaps one of the most crucial things to keep in mind when it comes to the tax implications of charitable giving, however, is "nonprofit" doesn't mean "tax-advantaged." The IRS keeps a long list of organizations that qualify for tax-deducted gifting in the Internal Revenue Code section 501I(3). Yet, many excellent nonprofits and civic organizations are not 501(c)(3)s. That doesn't mean you shouldn't give to them—truly, charity is *not* about tax deductions when it comes right down to it—it just means you shouldn't plan to include it as part of your tax-efficiency strategies.

Again, I would be remiss to not emphasize that these laws and definitions change year to year, so it is important to work with a team of qualified financial and tax professionals who can help you plan for the future and adjust to the times, in addition to verifying whether the charity you are considering is tax-exempt.

While impermanence seems to be a fixture of our tax system, one important aspect of charity tax law was made permanent for the foreseeable future. In 2015, Congress passed a budget deal signed into law by President Barack Obama. Among the provisions of the "Protecting Americans From Tax Hikes Act of 2015" were three key items that had been on charities' legislative "wish lists" for years:[67]

1. Wholesome food tax break — this allows farmers and non-corporate businesses to deduct donations of "wholesome" food to food banks and other charities.

2. Conservation easement tax break — encourages farmers, ranchers, loggers, and other landowners to set aside land for conservation efforts.

And, perhaps most widely applicable:

---

[67] Ashlea Ebeling. Forbes. Dec. 16, 2015. "Charities Laud Permanent Tax Breaks in House Deal."
https://www.forbes.com/sites/ashleaebeling/2015/12/16/charities-laud-permanent-tax-breaks-in-house-deal

3. IRA charitable rollovers — at age seventy-two, owners of traditional IRAs can make direct gifts of up to \$100,000 a year to a qualified charity directly from the IRA. This is known as a qualified charitable distribution, or QCD.

What makes permanent deduction No. 3 so important is a person who uses an IRA to contribute to charity in this way can:

1. Be charitable.
2. Avoid having their RMDs push them into a higher tax bracket by instead gifting them to those in need.
3. Take advantage of the tax-free aspect of a QCD when planning charitable gifting.
4. Potentially use the tax break to offset other tax consequences, like the tax on appreciated assets or capital gains. Please note, though, since the SECURE Act allows IRA contributions after an individual reaches age seventy-two, QCDs will be adversely affected (not all of the listed benefits will still apply) if a contribution is made to that IRA in the same year a QCD is withdrawn.[68]

Not only do we partner with our clients' tax advisors to guide them on how to make tax-efficient dontations, but if a client is looking for a good cause, we personally screen several mission organizations to learn which ones appear to be more effective and can make the biggest impact.

Planned Giving: After My Lifetime

For many charities, endowments and legacy gifts are the lifeblood that keeps them going. And, for many of us, a large final gift is an excellent way to continue a legacy of giving into perpetuity. The financial reasons for final charitable gifts, much

---

[68] Bob Carlson. Forbes. January 28,2020. "More Questions and Answers About the SECURE Act."
https://www.forbes.com/sites/bobcarlson/2020/01/28/more-questions-and-answers-about-the-secure-act/#113d49564869

like the annual contributions we often give, are many and, mostly, tax-based. A large final gift can be a good way to offload highly appreciated assets, allowing our favorite charities to experience the full use of an asset without us having to pay out a sizable tax bill.

Many charities have gone to great lengths to make this an attractive option, with some having preferences for certain donation types and strategies. For instance, many public entities, such as libraries and schools, have foundations to collect most of the donations and do major fundraising. Churches and universities often have special projects and intentional funding that stems from sizable endowments.

There are many financial vehicles to help you meet your charitable goals and give you benefits during your lifetime as well—from permanent life insurance policies to charitable trusts and charitable annuities. That's why it's important to plan ahead and work with a goal in mind. If you have some idea of what end you want to achieve, it can be easier to find the estate attorneys, tax professionals, and financial professionals who will be best qualified to help.

Non-Monetary Charitable Contributions

Ultimately, aside from the tax breaks, the good feeling, and the name on a park bench you might receive, your charitable contributions aren't about what you "get" in return. This is one other reason we should plan ahead for our good works; it's about doing the right thing.

Volunteering is one great, non-monetary way to support the charities and causes we believe in. Like I noted earlier, research shows retirees who are active and engaged volunteers in their communities often have a better sense of purpose and report more happiness than those who aren't. In volunteering, we have a reason to get up in the morning, and we meet new people and make friends. These are all things that may previously have stemmed from your nine-to-five workday but tend to fall by the wayside after leaving the workforce, making this consideration even more important.

We want to put the verse Mark 16: 15-16 into action, which is why we've chosen to support the community organizations we listed above.

Our families are one way we leave a legacy. But charitable giving—with our time, our talents, and our treasure—allows us to extend our legacies even further, beyond passing on Grandpa's nose or Grandma's ticklish feet.

CHAPTER 16

Avoiding Turbulence

As pilots or passengers prepare for take-off or landing, whether in a commercial or private aircraft, they rely on the guidance and direction given by the control tower for three things:

1. To keep them out of harm's way.
2. To provide instruction in accordance with safey regulations.
3. To get everyone where they're going as quickly as possible within the confines of numbers one and two.

Whether you manage your own financial plan or have an advisor, your order of priorities probably look similar to these.

One of the reasons I didn't name my practice after myself is because I believe the word "Falter" has no place on a business that is this critical to you. Clients need to develop trust and confidence that they'll avoid any nasty financial surprises. You would expect this thinking, even if a bit extreme, is a given across the industry. Statistics and actual events prove otherwise. Despite licensing, FINRA registrations, the Securities and Exchange Commission, the Office of the Comptroller of the Currency, state laws, and other oversight, retirement portfolios often nosedive. Sometimes they crash and burn.

As we demonstrated earlier, the security of the trillions of dollars Americans have invested in diverse retirement plans are of great concern not only to those who are invested but also to regulators who find themselves responsible for the consequences should the underlying products or investments encounter a downturn.

This is risky in this business. You're not usually shown all the information. Why would any advisor not make every effort to be transparent and a good teacher? In my opinion, the answer involves some "Monkey-see, monkey-do." It's an industry that has training that is not diversified and can best be described as incestuous, and yes there is greed too. New advisors are sometimes taught to find prospects and do what they can to sell to them; there is very little investment education. Many of these financial salespeople trust that their main office has all the answers, even though they don't even know the client. I don't have a crystal ball, but I know that and tailor client plans with this in mind.

Wall Street, including the subset, financial planning, is an entirely service-based business. There is nothing manufactured, no tires to kick, no fruit to squeeze, no price per pound to compare. Although I am among the breed that places clients' interests well ahead of my own, I am not pretending that the services coming from my business don't fall squarely as a service. How do you discern which service professional is competent and caring and who is just looking to cash in on a business which can be financially rewarding?

As with most businesses the more a representative sells or, the more fee-based clients they take on, the higher their individual income. The larger "chain store" Wall Street firms will take it a step further and reward more sales with extra bonuses. This incentivizes them to make a high number of client transactions. So, by design, each financial planner, especially at larger firms wants to open and fund your account, then quickly move on to bring in more. Many have taken an "off-the-rack" approach to financial plans. They ask a series of questions handed down from the big corporate office, they input the answers, and their computer tells them, "you need one of these, and three of those, and perhaps an optional one of these." Most representatives of these firms are discouraged from management to dig any deeper. They have maybe four pie charts with percentages of allocations and tell the client "this is what you need." If you open an account, they stay in touch but hand off the responsibility of filling your one-size-fits-most pie chart to back-office personnel far away in a big city someplace.

One of the red flags I look out for in a financial professional: Do they pitch products on the first meeting? Someone who does may be more interested in making a quick sale rather than getting to know you and recommending a path forward that meets your needs. I believe that advisors need to have the bulk of their money coming from planning trails; that way they have a vested interest in doing the right thing.

The Mid-American Difference

Seeing neighbors interact with my dad when I was growing up opened my eyes to the reality that people in his profession were instrumental in helping families plan for the financial challenges to come.

Now, I've been in the business for thirty-five years. I have my Series 65, and own our Registered Investment Advisory firm.

Retirement is more difficult today, with inflation running rampant and the possibility of taxes going up—I believe you need a financial advisor now more than ever. Because Mid-American Wealth is an independent firm, there is no obligation to offer products that benefit any specific carrier or company the way a national name brand firm might. The financial strategies I recommend aren't dictated by a home office, but rather, based on each clients' individual needs.

In essence, the difference is that we care. We not only say we put the clients' needs first, but we also put this into action. It is part of our planning process. Nearly half of our business comes from unsolicited referrals, so we have to be doing something right!

The goal is to not only be able to retire, but to be able to stay retired. We aim to produce enough income to allow a retiree to do this.

In my opinion, clients are best served with a "holistic approach." Remember, there is no "one-size-fits-all" plan for every single client. Each client, each family, and each situation is different. That was one of the very first lessons I learned from my father, and it was a large reason for his personal success.

Our main goal is to be on the same side of the desk as you are. When I sit down with a client in my office for a "one-on-one" first meeting, I am not sitting *behind* some large, designer-inspired executive desk; I am seated *with* them at a roundtable, to ensure that they feel comfortable speaking freely and openly. I do not want my clients to be awed by a fancy office; I want them to be frank and relaxed.

It is my hope that we will soon meet with you at that very table. Now that you've read through my general approaches to financial situations, I'd love to take a look at your specific individual situation and see how we can help you move into and through retirement with financial confidence and a sound strategy in place.

CHAPTER 17

Charting New Territory

"There are no shortcuts to any place worth going to."
— Irish Proverb

I started this book by sharing my vision of Middle America from the cockpit of a small private airplane flying over the fields and towns around my home in Kansas City. I invited you to come along on my journey from my childhood in West Virginia to my life today in the Heartland of America.

While working on this book, I also traveled far from home. I went to two of the most diverse locations on earth, New Zealand and Israel. The trip gave me the opportunity to see the world from an extreme diametric perspective. I flew 8,200 miles to the island nation of New Zealand and enjoyed the beauty and serenity of largely an unspoiled countryside. I felt the connection the people of New Zealand have with their land and their environment. I returned home to America with an awakened concern for the beauty of our land and a renewed commitment to the conservation of our precious resources.

A month later, I flew 6,500 miles in the opposite direction to the tiny nation-state of Israel. There, I was surrounded by the culture and religious diversity of one of the most historically important places on earth. I walked the ancient streets and dusty shorelines of places known to me from the Bible, I met scholars who immersed themselves in the study of ancient texts, the Torah, the Old Testament and who could debate the meaning of a single word or letter in those writings. I saw firsthand the cost of eternal vigilance and awareness, the reality of living day to day with the very real threat of terrorism. This time, I returned to the safety of the U.S. with a realization of the dangers which abound on other parts of the globe. I renewed my commitment to ensure the safety of my granddaughter and all children to live in a more peaceful place.

As a landowner, a hunter, a conservationist, and a herd manager, New Zealand impressed me with its thousands of acres of lush forest and pastures. There are beautiful vineyards, pastures of sheep and cattle, nearly unlimited natural resources, and abundant rainfall keeping everything green and growing. I can see the positive effect that years of careful management and positive advanced planning has brought to the successful management of those resources.

In Israel, the countryside is dry and dusty, it flourishes only when properly managed and irrigated, hunting is strictly limited, and in 2010, fishing on the Sea of Galilee was banned due to overfishing and low water levels. The vineyards must be irrigated and water must also be sent to the population centers. It can draw down all sources of freshwater to dangerously low levels.

In Israel, 8.79 million people are crammed onto 8,000 acres, giving it a population density of 377 per square kilometer. Compare that to New Zealand, where 4.6 million citizens share 104,000 acres, for a population density of only fifteen per square kilometer.

The citizens of Israel must live in constant contact and friction, with twenty-five times as many people as New Zealand. In addition to living in much closer proximity than most other nations, safety is also a common concern in Israel.

As I boarded the jet for my return flight to the heartland of the United States, I reflected on my week spent walking the ancient streets of Jerusalem and other parts of the Holy Land of Israel. It is impossible to come to this small nation and not be struck by the history and the reality of living in a land where each activity must be considered carefully, and daily survival is not simply taken for granted.

There are twenty-seven cities around the planet that are each home to more people than this nation of just 8.3 million residents. Forty-five of the states in America are larger than the entire nation of Israel. A billion people worldwide, twenty-two neighboring countries, and political opportunists around the world are all intent on the destruction of Israel. No other nation on earth stands against such odds, no other group faces this level of threat of extinction on a daily basis.

And yet, my time in Israel has validated my thoughts on the power of positive advance planning for future success and survival. I walked the ancient streets, I waded into the Sea of Galilee, and I touched the olive tree in the garden of Gethsemane. Everywhere I turned, there were locals watching over me and my companions, keeping each of us safe. Machne Yehuda Shuk, the centuries-old marketplace, teems with every race and religion, there is energy and enthusiasm as commerce and tradition merge, just as it has done for more than 1,000 years.

Israelis share their country with people from around the world, knowing that any one of the visitors could be a terrorist intent on their destruction, so they were vigilant and watchful. Every generation of Jew in Israel, and around the world, study their situation every single day. They assess the threats and the defenses available to them. They plan for survival.

In American history, this vigilant mindset among the Jews has been on display since the birth of our nation. Haym Salomon, a Polish immigrant, worked directly with General George Washington using his own wisdom, dedication, experience, and sacrifice to help finance the American Revolution.

Salomon was a broker and trader who specialized in negotiating the exchange of American currency bills for the currency of other countries in order to fund the American war effort. The loans Salomon secured were instrumental in helping Washington afford supplies and weapons and pay troops and mercenaries to keep fighting the British. By most accounts, it is estimated Salomon raised and loaned over $600,000 during the course of the war, and it was he who provided emergency funding for the pivotal battle of Yorktown, where Washington defeated General Cornwallis' British troops.[69]

In addition to the money raised and loaned to the war effort, Salomon also arranged the funding for the pensions for wounded soldiers and war veterans. He provided loans and lines of credit for James Madison and others who attended the Continental Congress so they could remain in Philadelphia to found this nation.

There is another American legend involving Salomon. At the beginning of the war, the British forces captured New York City in the middle of September 1776, intending to use the private homes in the city to garrison British troops. Washington had planned to burn much of the city to deny British forces the use of those homes, but Congress denied Washington the authority to do so.

Mysteriously, a few days later, nearly 500 homes did catch fire, representing nearly a quarter of the usable buildings in New York. Washington was quoted as saying, "Providence, or some good honest fellow, has done more for us than we were disposed to do for ourselves."

British general William Howe maintained that the Sons of Liberty were responsible and ordered all known members rounded up and jailed, including Salomon, who may have been involved in the plan to burn those homes. Most of the homes burned that night belonged to Loyalists, people who were willing to aid and provide shelter to the British troops. Others belonged to members of Sons of Liberty, who chose personal loss rather than aiding the British.

---

[69] Jewish Currents. January 6, 2018. "Financier of the Revolutionary War." https://jewishcurrents.org/financier-of-the-revolutionary-war

Perhaps in recognition of the actions Salomon took to prevent the forced billeting of soldiers in private homes in New York, Madison himself who wrote and introduced the third amendment to the Constitution of the United States: "No Soldier shall, in time of peace be quartered in any house, without the consent of the Owner, nor in time of war, but in a manner to be prescribed by law."

Ironic Symmetry

Just as Haym Salomon was the trusted confidant and advisor to George Washington and helped ensure both the success of the American Revolution and the birth of this Nation, I believe in the same values and objectives.

It is not enough to simply wave a flag and declare that you are an American. You must believe in the nation as a whole, you must have a positive plan for the future for you, your children, your grandchildren.

It is not enough to simply acquire a set amount of money by a specified date in order to claim your gold watch and retire; you must have a positive plan for your retirement. Studies have shown that people without a strong financial plan are 70 percent more likely to file bankruptcy within five years of winning the lottery. The same thing often happens to retirees who work and save for years, only to spend without purpose as soon as they retire.

It was not enough for Washington to have a battle plan to confront Cornwallis. He also needed the help and the wisdom of his friend Salomon to ensure the money he needed to achieve success would be available.

It was not enough for Madison and the delegates to the Constitutional Convention in Philadelphia to want freedom. They had to have a positive plan for this nation and the assistance of financial planners like Salomon to ensure financial stability for this well-planned nation of ours.

That is the message I wanted my first book to bring; an invitation for you to share with me your hopes and dreams for a secure retirement. Allow me the honor of reviewing your thoughts and answering your questions. Permit me to assist you in formulating the positive plan that will address your needs and the needs of your family.

Make your journey all it can possibly be.

About the Author

Mark Falter is the founder and president of Mid-American Wealth Advisory Group and has been in the financial services industry since 1984.

He is a host of the *Retirement Income Hour* radio show and has been featured on Fox Business channel, Fox4 News Kansas City, and the US Business Journal.

Mark has worked with seniors for most of his career, and is aware of the challenges facing retirees today. Mark created Mid-American Wealth Advisory Group Inc. as a financial management firm in Kansas City that specializes in helping retirees and pre-retirees build and preserve their wealth through asset management, tax strategies, and estate planning.

Mark is an Investment Adviser Representative and has previously worked at Investors Capital Advisory and Investors Capital Corporation.

You can meet Mark by requesting a consultation or attending one of his seminars in the Kansas City area.